Entertainment Director...

BEL...AST
GUIDEBOOK
2018

SHOPS, RESTAURANTS, ATTRACTIONS & NIGHTLIFE

The Most Positively
Reviewed and Recommended
by Locals and Travelers

EGP Editorial

BELFAST
GUIDEBOOK
2018

SHOPS, RESTAURANTS, ATTRACTIONS & NIGHTLIFE

BELFAST GUIDEBOOK 2018
Shops, Restaurants, Attractions & Nightlife

© George H. Erdrich, 2018
© E.G.P. Editorial, 2018

ISBN-13: 978-1986246248
ISBN-10: 1986246248

I N D E X

BELFAST GUIDEBOOK 2019

Shops, Restaurants, Attractions & Nightlife

This directory is dedicated to Besfast Business Owners and Managers
who provide the experience that the locals and tourists enjoy.
Thanks you very much for all that you do and thank for being the "People Choice".

Thanks to everyone that posts their reviews online and
the amazing reviews sites that make our life easier.

The places listed in this book are the most positively reviewed
and recommended by locals and travelers from around the world.

Thank you for your time and enjoy the directory that is
designed with locals and tourist in mind!

TOP 500 SHOPS

Recommended by Locals & Trevelers

(From #1 to #500)

#1
Avoca
Category: Home Decor
Average price: £26-45
Address: 41 Arthur Street
Belfast BT1 4GB, UK
Phone: +44 28 9027 9950

#2
Victoria Square
Category: Shopping Center
Average price: £26-45
Address: Victoria Square
Belfast BT1 4GQ, UK
Phone: +44 28 9032 2277

#3
Craftworld
Category: Arts & Crafts
Average price: £11-25
Address: 23-29 Queen Street
Belfast BT1 6EA, UK
Phone: +44 28 9024 9000

#4
Elliotts Fancy Dress
Category: Costumes
Average price: Under £10
Address: 110 Ann Street
Belfast BT1 3HH, UK
Phone: +44 28 9032 0532

#5
Alice's Wonderland for Gifts
Category: Home Decor,
Cards & Stationery, Gift Shop
Average price: £11-25
Address: College Street
Belfast BT1 6ET, UK
Phone: +44 28 9024 1342

#6
Forbidden Planet
Category: Hobby Shop
Average price: £11-25
Address: 52-54 Ann Street
Belfast BT1 4EG, UK
Phone: +44 28 9043 8744

#7
Forestside Shopping Centre
Category: Shopping Center
Average price: £11-25
Address: Upper Galwally
Belfast BT8 6FY, UK
Phone: +44 28 9049 4990

#8
Bradbury Graphics Art Store
Category: Art Supplies, Art Gallery
Average price: £11-25
Address: 1 - 2 Lyndon Court
Belfast BT1 6EF, UK
Phone: +44 28 9023 3535

#9
Miss Moran
Category: Tobacco Shop
Average price: £11-25
Address: 6 Church Lane
Belfast BT1 2, UK
Phone: +44 28 9024 6826

#10
No Alibis
Category: Bookstore
Average price: £11-25
Address: 83 Botanic Avenue
Belfast BT7 1JL, UK
Phone: +44 28 9031 9607

#11
Boots
Category: Drugstore
Address: Castle Court
Belfast BT1 1DD, UK
Phone: +44 28 9032 2803

#12
The Disney Store
Category: Toy Store
Average price: £11-25
Address: 11 Donegall Place
Belfast BT1 5AA, UK
Phone: +44 28 9024 6477

#13
Asia Supermarket
Category: Grocery, Wholesale Store
Average price: £11-25
Address: 189 Ormeau Road
Belfast BT7 1SQ, UK
Phone: +44 28 9032 6396

#14
Mike Hunt Clothing
Category: Fashion
Average price: Under £10
Address: High Street
Belfast BT1 2JZ, UK
Phone: +44 28 9031 4155

#15
Atelier
Category: Women's Clothing
Average price: £26-45
Address: 23 Queens Arcade
Belfast BT1 5FE, UK
Phone: +44 28 9027 8008

#16
IKEA Belfast
Category: Furniture Store,
Kitchen & Bath
Average price: £11-25
Address: 306 Airport Road West
Belfast BT3 9EJ, UK
Phone: +44 845 355 1113

#17
Lee Foods
Category: Grocery, Wholesale Store
Average price: Under £10
Address: 98-108 Donegall Pass
Belfast BT7 1BX, UK
Phone: +44 28 9024 8548

#18
The Wicker Man
Category: Arts & Crafts, Flowers & Gifts
Average price: £11-25
Address: 44-46 High Street
Belfast BT1 2BE, UK
Phone: +44 28 9024 3550

#19
Apple Store
Category: Computers
Average price: Above £46
Address: Victoria Square
Belfast BT1 4GQ, UK
Phone: +44 28 9016 1900

#20
Society of St Vincent De Paul
Category: Thrift Store
Average price: Under £10
Address: 196-200 Antrim Road
Belfast BT15 2, UK
Phone: +44 28 9035 1561

#21
Viva Retro
Category: Antiques,
Vintage & Consignment
Average price: £11-25
Address: 15 Lower North Street
Belfast BT1 1NA, UK
Phone: +44 7982 755058

#22
Little Heart
Category: Jewelry, Children's Clothing
Average price: £11-25
Address: 18 Queens Arcade
Belfast BT1 5FF, UK
Phone: +44 28 9032 0209

#23
Oxfam Books
Category: Thrift Store, Books,
Mags, Music & Video
Average price: Under £10
Address: 22 Rosemary Street
Belfast BT1 1QD, UK
Phone: +44 28 9032 0527

#24
Rusty Zip
Category: Vintage & Consignment
Average price: £11-25
Address: 28 Botanic Avenue
Belfast BT7 1JQ, UK
Phone: +44 28 9024 9700

#25
Fresh Garbage
Category: Fashion, Jewelry
Average price: £11-25
Address: 24 Rosemary Street
Belfast BT1 1QD, UK
Phone: +44 28 9024 2350

#26
Wyse Byse
Category: Department Store
Average price: Under £10
Address: 29-35 Cregagh Road
Belfast BT6 8PX, UK
Phone: +44 28 9045 0248

#27
Bedeck
Category: Home Decor
Average price: Above £46
Address: 465 Lisburn Road
Belfast BT9 7EZ, UK
Phone: +44 28 9066 9828

#28
Dunnes Store
Category: Department Store
Average price: Under £10
Address: 1-7 High Street
Belfast BT1 2AA, UK
Phone: +44 28 9041 7880

#29
Argento
Category: Jewelry
Average price: £11-25
Address: 11 Royal Avenue
Belfast BT1 1FB, UK
Phone: +44 28 9031 1059

#30
The Bookstore
Category: Bookstore
Average price: Under £10
Address: 21 Lower North Street
Belfast BT1 1LA, UK
Phone: +44 7939 315434

#31
HMV
Category: Books, Music & Video
Average price: £26-45
Address: Castle Place
Belfast BT1 1PT, UK
Phone: +44 843 221 0116

#32
Matchetts Musical Instruments
Category: Musical Instruments
Average price: £26-45
Address: 6 Wellington Place
Belfast BT1 6GE, UK
Phone: +44 28 9032 6695

#33
Liberty Blue
Category: Women's Clothing
Average price: £11-25
Address: 19-21 Lombard Street
Belfast BT1 1RB, UK
Phone: +44 28 9043 7745

#34
SS Moore Sports
Category: Sports Wear
Average price: £26-45
Address: 6-10 Chichester Street
Belfast BT1 4LA, UK
Phone: +44 28 9032 2966

#35
Early Learning Centre
Category: Toy Store
Average price: £26-45
Address: Unit 32 Castle Ct
Belfast BT1 1DD, UK
Phone: +44 28 9023 2344

#36
Game
Category: Videos & Game Rental, Hobby
Shop, Electronics, Computers
Average price: £26-45
Address: Castle Court
Belfast BT1 1DD, UK
Phone: +44 28 9024 2677

#37
Levi's Store
Category: Fashion
Average price: £11-25
Address: Victoria Square
Belfast BT1 4QG, UK
Phone: +44 28 9024 2955

#38
Willo
Category: Cards & Stationery, Jewelry
Average price: £11-25
Address: 387 Ormeau Road
Belfast BT7 2, UK
Phone: +44 28 9064 1222

#39
Urban Pharmacy
Category: Drugstore
Average price: £11-25
Address: 56 Dublin Road
Belfast BT2 7HN, UK
Phone: +44 28 9024 6336

#40
Gaby's
Category: Children's Clothing
Average price: £26-45
Address: 34 Gresham Street
Belfast BT1 1JN, UK
Phone: +44 28 9032 5139

#41
McCann's Army & Navy Store
Category: Hobby Shop
Average price: £11-25
Address: Unit 7/8
Belfast BT1 1JQ, UK
Phone: +44 28 9032 4297

#42
Semi-Chem
Category: Cosmetics & Beauty Supply
Average price: £11-25
Address: Castle Court
Belfast BT1 1DD, UK
Phone: +44 28 9023 6177

#43
Queen's Arcade
Category: Jewelry, Florist, Fashion
Average price: £26-45
Address: Royal Avenue
Belfast BT1 1, UK
Phone: +44 28 9024 9105

#44
Carroll's
Category: Flowers & Gifts
Average price: £11-25
Address: 2-6 Castle Pl
Belfast BT1 1GB, UK
Phone: +44 28 9023 8899

#45
Smyth's Irish Linens
Category: Fabric Store
Average price: £11-25
Address: 65-67 Royal Avenue
Belfast BT1 1FE, UK
Phone: +44 28 9024 2232

#46
Abacus Beads
Category: Arts & Crafts
Average price: Under £10
Address: 8 Castle St
Belfast BT1 1HB, UK
Phone: +44 28 9023 6087

#47
Oxfam Home
Category: Thrift Store
Average price: £11-25
Address: 52-54 Dublin Road
Belfast BT2 7HN, UK
Phone: +44 28 9032 5546

#48
Dorothy Perkins
Category: Women's Clothing
Average price: £11-25
Address: Unit 14 Castle Ct
Belfast BT1 1DD, UK
Phone: +44 28 9023 5270

#49
Doc Shop
Category: Shoe Store
Average price: £11-25
Address: 11 Pottinger's Entry
Belfast BT1 4DT, UK
Phone: +44 28 9031 3671

#50
Bookfinders
Category: Bookstore
Average price: £11-25
Address: 47 University Road
Belfast BT7 1ND, UK
Phone: +44 28 9032 8269

#51
Belfast Exposed
Category: Art Gallery
Average price: £11-25
Address: 23 Donegall Street
Belfast BT1 2FF, UK
Phone: +44 28 9031 4343

#52
Game Stop
Category: Computers
Average price: £11-25
Address: 9 Arthur St
Belfast BT1 4FD, UK
Phone: +44 28 9032 1847

#53
Surf Mountain
Category: Sporting Goods
Average price: £11-25
Address: 12 Brunswick Street
Belfast BT2 7GE, UK
Phone: +44 28 9024 8877

#54
Remus Uomo
Category: Men's Clothing
Average price: £26-45
Address: Unit 49 Castle Court
Belfast BT1 1DD, UK
Phone: +44 28 9032 0077

#55
Trade Winds
Category: Flowers & Gifts,
Arts & Crafts, Jewelry
Average price: £11-25
Address: 348 Lisburn Road
Belfast BT9 6GH, UK
Phone: +44 28 9066 3139

#56
Nicholas Gallery
Category: Art Gallery
Average price: Above £46
Address: 571A Lisburn Road
Belfast BT9 7GS, UK
Phone: +44 28 9068 7767

#57
Emer Gallery
Category: Art Gallery
Average price: £11-25
Address: 465-467 Antrim Road
Belfast BT15 3BJ, UK
Phone: +44 28 9077 8777

#58
Schuh
Category: Shoe Store
Average price: £26-45
Address: 33-39 Royal Avenue
Belfast BT1 1FD, UK
Phone: +44 28 9024 3756

#59
Accents Home & Gift
Category: Flowers & Gifts
Average price: £11-25
Address: 148 Lisburn Road
Belfast BT9 6AJ, UK
Phone: +44 28 9068 1200

#60
Past Times
Category: Flowers & Gifts, Home Decor
Average price: £11-25
Address: 48-50 Fountain Street
Belfast BT1 5EE, UK
Phone: +44 28 9031 2311

#61
China Craft
Category: Flowers & Gifts
Average price: £11-25
Address: 24 Queens Arcade
Belfast BT1 5FF, UK
Phone: +44 28 9023 0766

#62
Gamestop
Category: Videos & Game Rental
Address: 9 Arthur Sq
Belfast BT1 4, UK
Phone: +44 28 9032 1847

#63
Mr Pound
Category: Discount Store
Average price: £11-25
Address: 16 High Street
Belfast BT1 2BS, UK
Phone: +44 28 9033 2240

#64
The Perfume Shop
Category: Cosmetics & Beauty Supply
Average price: £11-25
Address: 1 Victoria Square
Belfast BT1 4, UK
Phone: +44 28 9023 5801

#65
Copper Moon
Category: Arts & Crafts, Jewelry
Average price: £26-45
Address: 1 Wellington Street
Belfast BT1 6HT, UK
Phone: +44 28 9023 5325

#66
Fat Face
Category: Fashion
Average price: £11-25
Address: 51-3 Fountain Street
Belfast BT1 5EA, UK
Phone: +44 28 9033 1812

#67
Spiral Threads
Category: Women's Clothing,
Men's Clothing, Arts & Crafts
Average price: £26-45
Address: 8 Pottinger's Entry
Belfast BT1 4DT, UK
Phone: +44 28 9024 6865

#68
Castle Court
Category: Shopping Center
Average price: £11-25
Address: Castle Court
Belfast BT1 1DD, UK
Phone: +44 28 9023 4591

#69
Cardland
Category: Cards & Stationery
Average price: Under £10
Address: 10 Castle Lane
Belfast BT1 5DA, UK
Phone: +44 28 9031 1821

#70
Lauren May
Category: Jewelry
Average price: £11-25
Address: 10 Queen's Arcade
Belfast BT1 5FF, UK
Phone: +44 28 9023 2681

#71
Richer Sounds
Category: Electronics
Average price: £11-25
Address: 5 Smithfield Square North
Belfast BT7 1AB, UK
Phone: +44 28 9032 1332

#72
Sports Direct
Category: Sports Wear, Hobby Shop
Average price: Under £10
Address: Boucher Retail Park Boucher
Crescent Belfast BT12 6HU, UK
Phone: +44 844 332 5667

#73
Office
Category: Shoe Store
Average price: £26-45
Address: 2 High Street
Belfast BT1 2AA, UK
Phone: +44 28 9023 5189

#74
Makro Wholesalers
Category: Wholesale Store,
Grocery, Department Store
Average price: Under £10
Address: 97 Kingsway
Belfast BT17 9NS, UK
Phone: +44 844 445 7445

#75
Bargain Books
Category: Bookstore
Average price: Under £10
Address: Unit 36 Castle Ct
Belfast BT1 1DD, UK
Phone: +44 28 9031 4154

#76
Debenhams Retail
Category: Department Store
Average price: Under £10
Address: Castle Court
Belfast BT1 1DD, UK
Phone: +44 844 561 6161

#77
Karen Millen
Category: Women's Clothing
Average price: £26-45
Address: 61-63 Donegall Place
Belfast BT1 5AG, UK
Phone: +44 28 9031 9096

#78
Games Workshop
Category: Books, Mags, Music & Video
Address: Castle Court
Belfast BT1 1DD, UK
Phone: +44 28 9023 3684

#79
Easons
Category: Bookstore
Average price: £11-25
Address: 20 Donegal Place
Belfast BT12 5, UK
Phone: +44 28 9023 5070

#80
Creations
Category: Furniture Store
Average price: £26-45
Address: 17-21 Bruce Street
Belfast BT2 7JD, UK
Phone: +44 28 9032 3197

#81
4urphone Mobile Phones
Category: Mobile Phones
Average price: £11-25
Address: 49a Rosemary Street
Belfast BT1 1FB, UK
Phone: +44 28 9032 3543

#82
H&M
Category: Women's Clothing,
Men's Clothing
Average price: Under £10
Address: Victoria Sq
Belfast BT1 4, UK
Phone: +44 28 9026 8070

#83
Remus Uomo
Category: Men's Clothing
Address: Victoria Square
Belfast BT1 4QG, UK
Phone: +44 28 9032 3777

#84
Muse
Category: Jewelry
Average price: £11-25
Address: CastleCourt Shopping Center
Belfast BT1 1DD, UK
Phone: +44 28 9023 4591

#85
Sheldon Framing
Category: Framing
Average price: £11-25
Address: 1a Donegall Square East
Belfast BT1 5HB, UK
Phone: +44 28 9032 4295

#86
Paperchase
Category: Cards & Stationery
Address: Unit 41 Victoria Square
Belfast BT1 4QG, UK
Phone: +44 844 800 3705

#87
House of Fraser
Category: Department Store
Average price: £26-45
Address: Victoria Square
Belfast BT1 4, UK
Phone: +44 844 800 3075

#88
Faith Mission
Category: Bookstore
Address: 5-7 Queen St
Belfast BT1 6EA, UK
Phone: +44 28 9023 3733

#89
Fossil
Category: Accessories
Average price: £26-45
Address: 22a Victoria Square
Belfast BT1 4QB, UK
Phone: +44 28 9026 8620

#90
Superdrug Store
Category: Drugstore
Average price: Under £10
Address: 21-23 Ann Street
Belfast BT1 4EA, UK
Phone: +44 28 9032 0400

#91
Leo
Category: Jewelry
Address: Castle Court
Belfast BT1 1DD, UK
Phone: +44 28 9024 6910

#92
Mama's & Papa's
Category: Baby Gear & Furniture
Average price: £26-45
Address: Victoria Square
Belfast BT1 4QG, UK
Phone: +44 845 268 2000

#93
Home Front Exhibition
Category: Art Gallery, Museum
Average price: Under £10
Address: 21 Talbot Street
Belfast BT1 2LD, UK
Phone: +44 28 9032 0392

#94
Golden Thread Gallery
Category: Art Gallery
Address: 84-94 Great Patrick Street
Belfast BT1 2LU, UK
Phone: +44 28 9033 0920

#95
Dawson Wright Hardware
Category: Hardware Store
Average price: £11-25
Address: 355 Woodstock Road
Belfast BT6 8PU, UK
Phone: +44 28 9045 0381

#96
Ideas In Furniture
Category: Furniture Store
Average price: Above £46
Address: 208 Lisburn Road
Belfast BT9 6GD, UK
Phone: +44 28 9038 1595

#97
L'Occitane
Category: Cosmetics & Beauty Supply
Average price: £26-45
Address: 24 Ann Street
Belfast BT1 4EF, UK
Phone: +44 28 9032 1422

#98
Blacks
Category: Outdoor Gear
Address: 18/22 Castle Place
Belfast BT1 1GB, UK
Phone: +44 28 9031 5947

#99
Joseph Rea & Co
Category: Jewelry
Average price: £11-25
Address: 76 Ann Street
Belfast BT1 4EH, UK
Phone: +44 28 9032 0477

#100
Victoria Gault
Category: Florist
Average price: £26-45
Address: Queens Arcade
Belfast BT1 3, UK
Phone: +44 28 9024 4746

#101
Size?
Category: Shoe Store
Average price: £11-25
Address: 9 Upper Queen Street
Belfast BT1 6FB, UK
Phone: +44 28 9032 1730

#102
Two Seasons
Category: Fashion
Average price: £11-25
Address: Victoria Square
Belfast BT1 4QB, UK
Phone: +44 28 9032 4525

#103
Bogart Boutique
Category: Men's Clothing
Average price: £26-45
Address: 4 Callander Street
Belfast BT1 5, UK
Phone: +44 28 9024 3508

#104
Cotswold
Category: Hobby Shop
Average price: £26-45
Address: 7-11 Castle Lane
Belfast BT1 5DB, UK
Phone: +44 28 9024 8607

#105
The Steensons
Category: Jewelry
Average price: £26-45
Address: Bedford Street
Belfast BT2 7FD, UK
Phone: +44 28 9024 8269

#106
McNeillys Jewellers
Category: Jewelry
Address: 7 Lombard Street
Belfast BT1 1RB, UK
Phone: +44 28 9032 6788

#107
Prestige Computers
Category: Electronics
Average price: £11-25
Address: 10 Pottingers Entry
Belfast BT1 4DT, UK
Phone: +44 28 9032 9014

#108
PS2
Category: Art Gallery
Address: 18 Donegall Street
Belfast BT1 2GP, UK
Phone: +44 28 9023 5912

#109
The Frameworks
Category: Art Gallery,
Cards & Stationery
Average price: £11-25
Address: 173 Ormeau Road
Belfast BT7 1SQ, UK
Phone: +44 28 9033 1394

#110
C S Suppliers
Category: Appliances
Average price: £11-25
Address: 118-122 Royal Avenue
Belfast BT1 1DL, UK
Phone: +44 28 9024 1181

#111
Hectors
Category: Hardware Store
Address: 243 Antrim Road
Belfast BT15 2GZ, UK
Phone: +44 28 9075 2908

#112
Build A Bear
Category: Toy Store
Average price: £26-45
Address: 16a Victoria Sq
Belfast BT1 4QB, UK
Phone: +44 28 9032 4458

#113
York Gate Shopping Centre
Category: Shopping Center
Average price: £11-25
Address: 100-150 York Gate Shopping
Centre Belfast BT15 1WA, UK
Phone: +44 28 9074 6978

#114
Apache
Category: Fashion
Average price: £11-25
Address: 46 Upper Queen St
Belfast BT1 6FD, UK
Phone: +44 28 9033 9985

#115
Harlequin Fancy Dress
Category: Costumes
Average price: £26-45
Address: 27 Botanic Ave
Belfast BT7 1JR, UK
Phone: +44 28 9023 1660

#116
Protocol
Category: Bridal
Average price: £11-25
Address: 216 Lisburn Road
Belfast BT9 6GD, UK
Phone: +44 28 9066 8645

#117
Deja Vu
Category: Vintage & Consignment
Average price: £11-25
Address: 453 Lisburn Road
Belfast BT9 7EY, UK
Phone: +44 28 9038 1807

#118
Engine Room Gallery
Category: Art Gallery
Average price: £26-45
Address: 414 Newtownards Road
Belfast BT4 1AB, UK
Phone: +44 28 9045 5184

#119
Smyth's Toystore
Category: Toy Store
Average price: £11-25
Address: Boucher Road
Belfast BT12 6HR, UK
Phone: +44 28 9038 2077

#120
Harrison
Category: Women's Clothing
Average price: £26-45
Address: 721 Lisburn Road
Belfast BT9 7GU, UK
Phone: +44 28 9066 6016

#121
Fiddlesticks
Category: Home Decor,
Furniture Store, Art Gallery
Average price: £11-25
Address: 9 Belmont Road
Belfast BT4 2AA, UK
Phone: +44 28 9065 5388

#122
Empathy Creations
Category: Jewelry
Average price: £11-25
Address: 12 E Bridge Street
Belfast BT7 2, UK
Phone: +44 28 9043 5704

#123
Cult Clothing
Category: Fashion
Average price: £26-45
Address: 75-87 Royal Ave
Belfast BT1 1FE, UK
Phone: +44 28 9024 0116

#124
Learning Space
Category: Hobby Shop
Average price: £11-25
Address: 11a Fountain Centre
Belfast BT1 6ET, UK
Phone: +44 28 9031 9360

#125
Zara, UK
Category: Fashion
Average price: £11-25
Address: 3 Donegall Pl
Belfast BT1 5AA, UK
Phone: +44 28 9044 5330

#126
Topshop
Category: Fashion
Average price: £26-45
Address: Victoria Sq
Belfast BT1 4, UK
Phone: +44 28 9032 3221

#127
Republic
Category: Fashion
Average price: Above £46
Address: Royal Avenue
Belfast BT1 1DD, UK
Phone: +44 28 9033 2481

#128
Urban Outfitters
Category: Women's Clothing
Average price: £26-45
Address: 43-55 Ann St
Belfast BT1 4ED, UK
Phone: +44 28 9043 6780

#129
Castle D I Y
Category: Keys & Locksmiths,
Hardware Store
Address: 363/365 Antrim Road
Belfast BT15 3BG, UK
Phone: +44 28 9074 1418

#130
Creative Cakes
Category: Shopping
Average price: £11-25
Address: 277 Upper Newtownards Road
Belfast BT4 3JF, UK
Phone: +44 28 9047 3391

#131
Matalan
Category: Fashion
Average price: £11-25
Address: Boucher Road
Belfast BT12 6HR, UK
Phone: +44 28 9068 6960

#132
Art and Hobby Store
Category: Art Supplies
Average price: £11-25
Address: Victoria Square Ctr
Belfast BT1 4LS, UK
Phone: +44 28 9033 2540

#133
Spinning Wheel
Category: Shades & Blinds,
Fabric Store, Hobby Shop
Average price: £11-25
Address: 9 Donegall Square West
Belfast BT1 6JH, UK
Phone: +44 28 9032 6111

#134
Conswater Shopping Centre
Category: Shopping Center
Average price: Under £10
Address: 1 Connswater Shopping Centre
Belfast BT5 5LP, UK
Phone: +44 28 9045 0111

#135
The Celtic Collection
Category: Sporting Goods, Soccer
Average price: £26-45
Address: 30 Ann St
Belfast BT1 4EG, UK
Phone: +44 28 9023 9111

#136
Matchetts Music Piano Shop
Category: Musical Instruments
Average price: £26-45
Address: Bedford Street
Belfast BT2 7FD, UK
Phone: +44 28 9023 3039

#137
The Corium
Category: Fashion, Jewelry
Average price: Under £10
Address: 37 Church Ln
Belfast BT1 4QN, UK
Phone: +44 28 9032 0813

#138
Cash Converters (UK)
Category: Pawn Shop
Average price: £11-25
Address: 22 High Street
Belfast BT1 2BD, UK
Phone: +44 28 9032 2622

#139
Electronic Centre
Category: Appliances
Average price: £26-45
Address: 16 College Sq E
Belfast BT1 6DE, UK
Phone: +44 28 9032 7357

#140
The Watch Store
Category: Watches
Average price: £26-45
Address: Queen's Arcade
Belfast BT1 3, UK
Phone: +44 28 9033 2250

#141
TK Maxx
Category: Discount Store
Average price: £11-25
Address: Donegal Arcade
Belfast BT1 1GA, UK
Phone: +44 28 9033 1151

#142
Evans
Category: Women's Clothing
Average price: Above £46
Address: Unit 59 Castle Court
Belfast BT1 1DD, UK
Phone: +44 28 9023 4960

#143
New Look
Category: Women's Clothing
Average price: £11-25
Address: Donegall Road
Belfast BT12 6HN, UK
Phone: +44 28 9043 7540

#144
Munn's Hardware
Category: Hardware Store
Average price: £11-25
Address: 531 Lisburn Road
Belfast BT9 7GQ, UK
Phone: +44 28 9038 1057

#145
Clockwork Orange
Category: Women's Clothing,
Men's Clothing
Average price: £26-45
Address: Victoria Square
Belfast BT1 6GQ, UK
Phone: +44 28 9032 0298

#146
Posh Frocks
Category: Women's Clothing
Average price: £26-45
Address: 673 Lisburn Rd
Belfast BT9 7GT, UK
Phone: +44 28 9066 7966

#147
Space NK
Category: Shopping
Address: 5 - 6 Donegall Square North
Belfast BT1 5GB, UK
Phone: +44 28 9033 0833

#148
Fred J Malcolm
Category: Jewelry
Average price: £26-45
Address: 18 Chichester St
Belfast BT1 4LB, UK
Phone: +44 28 9032 1491

#149
Place
Category: Art Gallery
Average price: Under £10
Address: 40 Fountain Street
Belfast BT1 5EE, UK
Phone: +44 28 9023 2524

#150
O'Neills Sportswear
Category: Sports Wear
Average price: £11-25
Address: 564-568 Falls Road
Belfast BT11 9AE, UK
Phone: +44 28 9062 2226

#151
Aldo
Category: Shoe Store
Average price: £26-45
Address: 12 Donegall Pl
Belfast BT1 5AA, UK
Phone: +44 28 9031 2843

#152
Loko
Category: Sporting Goods
Average price: £26-45
Address: 30 Gresham St
Belfast BT1 1JN, UK
Phone: +44 28 9031 0921

#153
Boots Store
Category: Drugstore
Average price:
Address: Unit 26-27 Castle Ct
Belfast BT1 1DD, UK
Phone: +44 28 9032 2803

#154
Burton
Category: Men's Clothing
Average price: £11-25
Address: Unit 14 Castle Court
Belfast BT1 1DD, UK
Phone: +44 28 9023 5276

#155
Furniture Emporium
Category: Furniture Store
Average price: £11-25
Address: 177 Donegall Street
Belfast BT1 2FJ, UK
Phone: +44 28 9031 0588

#156
Kennedy Florist
Category: Florist
Average price: Under £10
Address: 183 Donegall St
Belfast BT1 2FJ, UK
Phone: +44 28 9032 1587

#157
Poundland
Category: Discount Store
Average price: Under £10
Address: Castle Court Royal Ave
Belfast BT1 1DD, UK
Phone: +44 28 9023 8828

#158
Glass Slipper
Category: Shopping
Average price: £11-25
Address: 217 Woodstock Road
Belfast BT6 8PQ, UK
Phone: +44 28 9045 1333

#159
Fulton's
Category: Home & Garden
Average price: Above £46
Address: Boucher Plaza
Belfast BT12 6HR, UK
Phone: +44 28 9038 4700

#160
War On Want
Category: Bookstore, Thrift Store
Average price: Under £10
Address: 24 Botanic Avenue
Belfast BT7 1JQ, UK
Phone: +44 28 9024 7773

#161
New Look
Category: Fashion
Average price: £26-45
Address: 19 Donegall Pl
Belfast BT1 5AB, UK
Phone: +44 28 9089 7680

#162
Patchwork Goose
Category: Fabric Store
Average price: Under £10
Address: 341 Antrim Road
Belfast BT15 2HF, UK
Phone: +44 28 9035 1465

#163
Brian Keenan Guitar Centre
Category: Musical Instruments
Average price: £11-25
Address: 473 Lisburn Road
Belfast BT9 7EZ, UK
Phone: +44 28 9066 0504

#164
Vodafone Retail
Category: Mobile Phones
Average price: Under £10
Address: Unit 27
Belfast BT8 6FX, UK
Phone: +44 28 9064 0009

#165
Smyth & Gibson
Category: Men's Clothing
Average price: £26-45
Address: 16-22 Bedford Street
Belfast BT2 7GX, UK
Phone: +44 28 9023 0388

#166
Paragon Fabrics
Category: Fabric Store, Hobby Shop
Average price: £11-25
Address: 86 Donegall Pass
Belfast BT7 1BX, UK
Phone: +44 28 9033 1612

#167
Quiksilver
Category: Men's Clothing
Address: Castle Court Shopping Ctr
Belfast BT1 1, UK
Phone: +44 28 9033 2232

#168
Townhouse Gallery
Category: Art Gallery, Framing
Average price: £11-25
Address: 125 Great Victoria Street
Belfast BT2 7AH, UK
Phone: +44 28 9031 1798

#169
My Old Toy Box
Category: Hobby Shop
Average price: £11-25
Address: Smithfield Market
Belfast BT1 1JQ, UK
Phone: +44 7719 100483

#170
Smithfield Market
Category: Shopping Center
Average price: £11-25
Address: Smithfield
Belfast BT1 1JQ, UK
Phone: +44 28 9032 3248

#171
Margaret Forbes Jewellery
Category: Jewelry
Average price: £26-45
Address: 8 Arthur St
Belfast BT1 4GD, UK
Phone: +44 28 9024 3690

#172
Hallmark
Category: Cards & Stationery
Address: 5a College St
Belfast BT1 6ET, UK
Phone: +44 28 9024 1625

#173
Beaverbrooks The Jewellers
Category: Jewelry
Average price: Above £46
Address: 24 Donegall Place
Belfast BT1 5BA, UK
Phone: +44 28 9032 7066

#174
Joseph Rea
Category: Jewelry
Average price: £11-25
Address: 32 Castle Lane
Belfast BT1 5DB, UK
Phone: +44 28 9023 1122

#175
Cartridge World
Category: Office Equipment
Address: 32 Castle Street
Belfast BT1 1HB, UK
Phone: +44 28 9043 4331

#176
Oxfam Fair Trade
Category: Fabric Store, Jewelry
Address: 16 Rosemary Street
Belfast BT1 1QD, UK
Phone: +44 28 9024 7168

#177
Joseph Braddell & Sons
Category: Sporting Goods
Address: 11 North Street
Belfast BT1 1NA, UK
Phone: +44 28 9032 0525

#178
Ted Baker
Category: Men's Clothing
Address: Victoria Square
Belfast BT1 4, UK
Phone: +44 28 9032 4798

#179
Work Rest Play Interiors
Category: Office Equipment
Average price: £26-45
Address: 70-74 Donegall Street
Belfast BT1 2GU, UK
Phone: +44 28 9031 4303

#180
Cathedral Graphics
Category: Art Supplies
Average price: £11-25
Address: 62 Donegall St
Belfast BT1 2GT, UK
Phone: +44 28 9024 4082

#181
Gallery 73
Category: Art Gallery
Address: 73 Royal Avenue
Belfast BT1 1, UK
Phone: +44 7749 457860

#182
Belfast Print Workshop
Category: Art Schools, Art Gallery
Address: Waring Street
Belfast BT1 2ED, UK
Phone: +44 28 9023 1323

#183
Gowdys Menswear
Category: Men's Clothing
Average price: £11-25
Address: 121-131 Woodstock Road
Belfast BT6 8AB, UK
Phone: +44 28 9045 9052

#184
Northen Ireland Hospice Shop
Category: Thrift Store
Average price: Under £10
Address: 279 Ormeau Road
Belfast BT7 3GG, UK
Phone: +44 28 9064 1599

#185
Mcmullans Pharmacy
Category: Drugstore
Average price: £26-45
Address: 165 Lisburn Road
Belfast BT9 7AJ, UK
Phone: +44 28 9038 1882

#186
Threads
Category: Shades & Blinds, Jewelry,
Vintage & Consignment
Address: 289 Ormeau Road
Belfast BT7 3GG, UK
Phone: +44 28 9020 2838

#187
Beauty Basement
Category: Cosmetics & Beauty Supply
Average price: £11-25
Address: 7-9 Chichester Street
Belfast BT1 4JA, UK
Phone: +44 28 9023 6476

#188
Reids Florist
Category: Florist
Address: 154 Lisburn Road
Belfast BT9 6AJ, UK
Phone: +44 28 9066 3381

#189
Ellisons
Category: Jewelry
Average price: £11-25
Address: 3a The Fountain Centre
Belfast BT1 6ET, UK
Phone: +44 28 9032 5320

#190
Serenity Games
Category: Hobby Shop
Address: 46 Botanic Avenue
Belfast BT7 1JR, UK
Phone: +44 28 9024 9578

#191
Catalyst Arts Gallery
Category: Art Gallery
Average price: Under £10
Address: 5 College Court
Belfast BT1 6BS, UK
Phone: +44 28 9031 3303

#192
Jaeger Group
Category: Fashion
Average price: Above £46
Address: 25 Royal Avenue
Belfast BT1 1FB, UK
Phone: +44 28 9032 1438

#193
Mac Cosmetics
Category: Cosmetics & Beauty Supply
Address: Royal Avenue
Belfast BT1 1DD, UK
Phone: +44 28 9043 5546

#194
Molton Brown Emporium
Category: Cosmetics & Beauty Supply
Address: 16 Donegall Square North
Belfast BT1 5GB, UK
Phone: +44 28 9024 6674

#195
Fired Earth Interiors
Category: Home Decor
Average price: £26-45
Address: 180 Lisburn Rd
Belfast BT9 6AL, UK
Phone: +44 28 9023 8000

#196
Stephen Shaw Gallery
Category: Art Gallery
Address: 13 Winetavern Street
Belfast BT1 1JE, UK
Phone: +44 7901 814848

#197
H Samuel
Category: Jewelry
Address: 6 Castle Court
Belfast BT1 1DD, UK
Phone: +44 28 9043 5618

#198
E H Services
Category: Appliances
Address: 430 Woodstock Road
Belfast BT6 9DR, UK
Phone: +44 28 9045 4363

#199
Miss Selfridge
Category: Women's Clothing
Average price: £11-25
Address: 3 Castle Ct
Belfast BT1 1DD, UK
Phone: +44 28 9023 5008

#200
Cruise
Category: Fashion
Average price: Above £46
Address: Victoria Sq
Belfast BT1 4QG, UK
Phone: +44 28 9032 0550

#201
Tom West
Category: Framing
Average price: £11-25
Address: 264 Woodstock Road
Belfast BT6 9DN, UK
Phone: +44 28 9045 8728

#202
Mplex
Category: Computers
Address: 11 Dargan Road
Belfast BT3 9JU, UK
Phone: +44 28 9077 2999

#203
In Shop
Category: Shopping
Average price: Under £10
Address: High Street
Belfast BT1 2JZ, UK
Phone: +44 28 9032 9719

#204
Blush
Category: Bridal
Average price: £26-45
Address: 166 Lisburn Road
Belfast BT9 7, UK
Phone: +44 28 9066 1101

#205
American Golf Discount Centre
Category: Home & Garden
Address: 3 Connswater Link
Belfast BT5 5DL, UK
Phone: +44 28 9046 6688

#206
Crossins Chemist
Category: Drugstore
Address: 267 Antrim Road
Belfast BT15 2HR, UK
Phone: +44 28 9035 1084

#207
Medicare Chemists
Category: Drugstore
Average price: £11-25
Address: 483 Ormeau Road
Belfast BT7 3GR, UK
Phone: +44 28 9049 1512

#208
Union Jack Shop
Category: Shopping
Address: 354 Newtownards Road
Belfast BT4 1HG, UK
Phone: +44 28 9059 2909

#209
Medicare
Category: Drugstore
Address: 366a Lisburn Road
Belfast BT9 6GL, UK
Phone: +44 28 9066 7177

#210
The Antique Gallery
Category: Antiques
Average price: Above £46
Address: 505 Lisburn Road
Belfast BT9 7EZ, UK
Phone: +44 28 9066 3672

#211
McGrath
Category: Office Equipment
Address: 561 Lisburn Road
Belfast BT9 7GQ, UK
Phone: +44 28 9066 1199

#212
Arabesque Shoes
Category: Shoe Store
Average price: £26-45
Address: 60 Bloomfield Avenue
Belfast BT5 5AD, UK
Phone: +44 28 9045 9498

#213
Raspberry Beret
Category: Vintage & Consignment
Address: 111 Bloomfield Avenue
Belfast BT5 5AB, UK
Phone: +44 28 9045 6216

#214
Bargain Books
Category: Books, Mags, Music & Video
Average price: Under £10
Address: Unit 33
Belfast BT5 5LP, UK
Phone: +44 28 9046 1454

#215
Warnocks
Category: Department Store
Average price: £26-45
Address: 791-793 Lisburn Road
Belfast BT9 7GX, UK
Phone: +44 28 9038 1828

#216
Quiz Clothing
Category: Women's Clothing
Average price: £11-25
Address: Unit 11 Castle Ct
Belfast BT1 1DD, UK
Phone: +44 28 9032 1601

#217
Smyths Toys
Category: Toy Store
Average price: £11-25
Address: Unit 3-4 Drumkeen Retail Park
Bradford Court Belfast BT8 6RB, UK
Phone: +44 28 9064 6660

#218
Dundela Pharmacy
Category: Drugstore
Average price: £11-25
Address: 17-19 Belmont Road
Belfast BT4 2AA, UK
Phone: +44 28 9065 7853

#219
TJ Hughes
Category: Department Store
Average price: Under £10
Address: York Street
Belfast BT15 1WA, UK
Phone: +44 28 9074 1379

#220
GameTheWorld
Category: Videos & Games Rental,
Internet Cafe
Address: 801 lisburn road
Belfast BT9 7GX, UK
Phone: +44 28 9066 7559

#221
Direct Furniture
Category: Furniture Store
Average price: £11-25
Address: 595 Falls Road
Belfast BT11 9AB, UK
Phone: +44 28 9062 3930

#222
All Direct Furniture
Category: Furniture Store
Average price: £11-25
Address: Falls Road
Belfast BT11 9AB, UK
Phone: +44 28 9062 3362

#223
Pull & Bear
Category: Fashion
Average price: £11-25
Address: Victoria Sq
Belfast BT1 4QG, UK
Phone: +44 28 9031 6160

#224
Laura Ashley
Category: Fashion
Average price: £26-45
Address: Castle Ct
Belfast BT1 1DD, UK
Phone: +44 28 9023 3313

#225
Superdrug Store
Category: Drugstore
Average price: £11-25
Address: 48 Kennedy Way
Belfast BT11 9AP, UK
Phone: +44 28 9061 1243

#226
Stiletto Alternative Clothing
Category: Fashion
Average price: £11-25
Address: 17 Fountain Street
Belfast BT1 5EA, UK
Phone: +44 28 9024 7233

#227
Ann Summers
Category: Lingerie
Average price: Above £46
Address: 51 Rosemary Street
Belfast BT1 1QB, UK
Phone: +44 870 053 4017

#228
Patrick Collins & Co
Category: Furniture Store
Address: 140-144 Andersonstown Road
Belfast BT11 9BY, UK
Phone: +44 28 9061 2717

#229
Chef Shop
Category: Shopping
Average price: Above £46
Address: 29 Bruce St
Belfast BT2 7JD, UK
Phone: +44 28 9032 9200

#230
Topman
Category: Men's Clothing
Address: Victoria Square
Belfast BT1 4GQ, UK
Phone: +44 28 9032 3221

#231
Warehouse
Category: Women's Clothing
Average price: £11-25
Address: Castle Court
Belfast BT1 1DD, UK
Phone: +44 28 9043 9606

#232
Fonemedics
Category: Mobile Phones
Address: 33A Royal Avenue
Belfast BT1 1FD, UK
Phone: +44 28 9031 1081

#233
Space CRAFT
Category: Art Gallery
Average price: £11-25
Address: 9b The Fountain Centre
Belfast BT1 6ET, UK
Phone: +44 28 9032 9342

#234
Kavanagh Engravers
Category: Gift Shop
Average price: Above £46
Address: 36 Gresham Street
Belfast BT1 1JN, UK
Phone: +44 28 9032 5000

#235
Sew & Sew
Category: Fabric Store
Average price: Under £10
Address: High Street
Belfast BT1 2JZ, UK
Phone: +44 28 9058 3900

#236
Au Naturale
Category: Gift Shop
Address: Castle Ct
Belfast BT1 1DD, UK
Phone: +44 28 9023 9795

#237
Flexa
Category: Furniture Store
Average price: £11-25
Address: Castle Ct
Belfast BT1 1DD, UK
Phone: +44 28 9023 8822

#238
Cotton Print Factory Shop
Category: Fabric Store
Average price: £11-25
Address: 16-18 Dargan Crescent
Belfast BT3 9JP, UK
Phone: +44 28 9077 3893

#239
Finaghy News
Category: Newspapers & Magazines
Average price: £11-25
Address: 139 Upper Lisburn Road
Belfast BT10 0LH, UK
Phone: +44 28 9043 1122

#240
Peacocks Store
Category: Department Store
Average price: Under £10
Address: Connswater Shopping Centre
Belfast BT4 1HD, UK
Phone: +44 28 9046 0475

#241
Decathlon
Category: Sporting Goods
Average price: Under £10
Address: Holywood Exchange Retail Park
Belfast BT3 9EJ, UK
Phone: +44 28 9042 2049

#242
French Connection
Category: Fashion
Average price: £26-45
Address: 26-28 Corn Market
Belfast BT1 4DD, UK
Phone: +44 28 9024 6799

#243
Argos
Category: Discount Store
Average price: £11-25
Address: 53 Royal Avenue
Belfast BT1 1FD, UK
Phone: +44 845 165 7217

#244
GD1
Category: Accessories
Average price: £26-45
Address: College Street
Belfast BT1 6BT, UK
Phone: +44 28 9024 5250

#245
River Island
Category: Fashion
Address: Victoria Sq
Belfast BT1 4QG, UK
Phone: +44 28 9032 2463

#246
Exhibit
Category: Fashion
Average price: Under £10
Address: Unit 45 Castle Court
Belfast BT1 1DD, UK
Phone: +44 28 9023 4950

#247
Clinton Cards
Category: Cards & Stationery
Average price: £11-25
Address: Castle Ct
Belfast BT1 1DD, UK
Phone: +44 28 9043 9777

#248
Clinton Cards
Category: Cards & Stationery
Address: 5 Wellington Place
Belfast BT1 6GA, UK
Phone: +44 28 9032 8622

#249
All Sports
Category: Sporting Goods
Average price: £26-45
Address: 72 Stranmillis Road
Belfast BT9 5AD, UK
Phone: +44 28 9038 1722

#250
Sony Centre
Category: Electronics
Average price: £11-25
Address: 1 Donegall Square West
Belfast BT1 6JA, UK
Phone: +44 28 9543 8363

#251
Barratt Shoes
Category: Shoe Store
Average price: £26-45
Address: Unit 31 Castle Ct
Belfast BT1 1DD, UK
Phone: +44 28 9023 5562

#252
Baby Gap
Category: Children's Clothing
Average price: £11-25
Address: Unit 10 Castle Court
Belfast BT1 1DD, UK
Phone: +44 28 9032 8867

#253
TK Maxx
Category: Fashion
Average price: £11-25
Address: Boucher CR
Belfast BT12 6HU, UK
Phone: +44 28 9068 3808

#254
The Shed Factory
Category: Furniture Store
Address: 301 Glen Road
Belfast BT11 8BU, UK
Phone: +44 28 9061 6868

#255
James Wray Company
Category: Art Gallery
Average price: Above £46
Address: 14-16 James St South
Belfast BT2 7GA, UK
Phone: +44 28 9031 3013

#256
Harrison Healthcare
Category: Drugstore
Average price: £11-25
Address: 40 Donegall Pass
Belfast BT7 1BS, UK
Phone: +44 28 9032 0059

#257
Ferguson Flowers International
Category: Florist
Average price: £26-45
Address: 18 Wellington Place
Belfast BT1 6GE, UK
Phone: +44 28 9024 0111

#258
Claire's Accessories
Category: Accessories
Average price: Under £10
Address: Castle Ct
Belfast BT1 1DD, UK
Phone: +44 28 9024 6911

#259
Evangelical Bookshop
Category: Bookstore
Average price: £11-25
Address: 15 College Square East
Belfast BT1 6DD, UK
Phone: +44 28 9032 0529

#260
The Scout Shop Camp & Ski Centre
Category: Outdoor Gear
Average price: £11-25
Address: 12-14 College Square East
Belfast BT1 6DD, UK
Phone: +44 28 9032 0580

#261
Boots Store
Category: Drugstore
Address: 35-47 Donegall Place
Belfast BT1 5AW, UK
Phone: +44 28 9024 2332

#262
Jack & Jones
Category: Men's Clothing
Address: 11 Arthur St
Belfast BT1 4GA, UK
Phone: +44 28 9031 4441

#263
Jigsaw Womens Wear
Category: Women's Clothing
Average price: £26-45
Address: 12-14 Arthur St
Belfast BT1 4GA, UK
Phone: +44 28 9024 9110

#264
Reid's Shoes
Category: Shoe Store
Address: 111-119 Sandy Row
Belfast BT12 5ET, UK
Phone: +44 28 9024 4501

#265
Blacks
Category: Outdoor Gear
Average price: £11-25
Address: 18-22 Castle Pl
Belfast BT1 1, UK
Phone: +44 28 9031 5947

#266
Lunn's
Category: Jewelry
Average price: £11-25
Address: 1 Victoria Sq
Belfast BT1 4QG, UK
Phone: +44 28 9032 5250

#267
Tiso
Category: Outdoor Gear
Average price: £26-45
Address: 12-14 Corn Market
Belfast BT1 4DD, UK
Phone: +44 28 9023 1230

#268
Bogart
Category: Men's Clothing
Address: 57-59 Ann St
Belfast BT1 4EE, UK
Phone: +44 28 9023 1108

#269
St.
Category: Thrift Store
Average price: Under £10
Address: 138 Ormeau Road
Belfast BT7 2EB, UK
Phone: +44 28 9024 7699

#270
Hugo Boss
Category: Men's Clothing
Average price: £26-45
Address: Victoria Sq
Belfast BT1 4QG, UK
Phone: +44 28 9032 0550

#271
TM Lewin
Category: Men's Clothing
Average price: £26-45
Address: Victoria Sq
Belfast BT1 4, UK
Phone: +44 28 9024 1169

#272
Marks & Spencer
Category: Department Store
Average price: £11-25
Address: 48-52 Donegall Place
Belfast BT1 5BY, UK
Phone: +44 28 9023 5235

#273
Mooney's Pharmacy
Category: Drugstore
Address: 23-25 Clifton Street
Belfast BT13 1AD, UK
Phone: +44 28 9024 5033

#274
La Femme
Category: Women's Clothing
Address: 240 Ormeau Road
Belfast BT7 2FZ, UK
Phone: +44 28 9064 8131

#275
Cheepers
Category: Discount Store
Average price: Under £10
Address: 382-386 Woodstock Rd
Belfast BT6 8AB, UK
Phone: +44 28 9080 6860

#276
Paper Wishes
Category: Cards & Stationery
Address: 6 Cregagh Rd
Belfast BT6 9EP, UK
Phone: +44 28 9045 1784

#277
Beverly Hills
Category: Women's Clothing
Average price: Above £46
Address: 473 Lisburn Road
Belfast BT9 7, UK
Phone: +44 7742 931877

#278
DV8
Category: Fashion
Average price: £26-45
Address: 23 Castle Pl
Belfast BT1 1FY, UK
Phone: +44 28 9023 5556

#279
Ink World
Category: Office Equipment
Average price: £11-25
Address: 92 Bloomfield Ave
Belfast BT5 5LU, UK
Phone: +44 28 9029 2000

#280
Semi-Chem
Category: Cosmetics & Beauty Supply
Average price: Under £10
Address: Bloomfield Avenue
Belfast BT5 5LP, UK
Phone: +44 28 9045 4598

#281
Lulu Blu
Category: Women's Clothing
Average price: £26-45
Address: Bloomfield Ave
Belfast BT5 5AD, UK
Phone: +44 28 9045 0400

#282
Burton
Category: Men's Clothing
Address: Boucher Retail Park Boucher
Crescent Belfast BT12 6HR, UK
Phone: +44 28 9066 0995

#283
Orchid Lingerie
Category: Lingerie
Average price: £26-45
Address: 663 Lisburn Road
Belfast BT9 7GT, UK
Phone: +44 28 9038 1313

#284
Dune Footwear
Category: Shoe Store
Average price: £26-45
Address: Castle Court
Belfast BT1 1DD, UK
Phone: +44 28 9024 0725

#285
Yankee Store
Category: Flowers & Gifts, Home Decor
Average price: £26-45
Address: Unit 40 Castle Ct
Belfast BT1 1DD, UK
Phone: +44 28 9024 5285

#286
Rojo Ladies Shoes
Category: Women's Clothing
Average price: £26-45
Address: 613 Lisburn Road
Belfast BT9 7GT, UK
Phone: +44 28 9066 6998

#287
Sally Hair & Beauty Supplies
Category: Cosmetics & Beauty Supply
Address: 81-83 Boucher Rd
Belfast BT12 6HR, UK
Phone: +44 28 9066 9846

#288
Up & Running Ni
Category: Sports Wear
Average price: £11-25
Address: 60 Wellington Place
Belfast BT1 6GF, UK
Phone: +44 28 9032 5151

#289
Wallis Fashion Group
Category: Women's Clothing
Average price: £11-25
Address: 18-22 Castle Place
Belfast BT1 1GB, UK
Phone: +44 28 9032 6838

#290
Specsavers
Category: Eyewear & Opticians
Average price: £11-25
Address: 36-40 Ann St
Belfast BT1 4EG, UK
Phone: +44 28 9031 1999

#291
Swarovski Store
Category: Accessories
Average price: £26-45
Address: 39 Castle Lane
Belfast BT1 5DB, UK
Phone: +44 28 9031 1200

#292
Music Matters
Category: Musical Instruments
Average price: £11-25
Address: 20-22 Bradbury Place
Belfast BT7 1RS, UK
Phone: +44 28 9024 2335

#293
Harry Corry
Category: Home Decor
Average price: Under £10
Address: 49 Royal Ave
Belfast BT1 1FD, UK
Phone: +44 28 9032 0721

#294
Card Land
Category: Cards & Stationery
Average price: Under £10
Address: Castle Court
Belfast BT1 1DD, UK
Phone: +44 28 9031 2444

#295
NV
Category: Women's Clothing
Average price: Under £10
Address: Castle Court
Belfast BT1 1DD, UK
Phone: +44 28 9023 3383

#296
Just For You
Category: Gift Shop
Average price: £11-25
Address: 13 Belmont Road
Belfast BT4 2AA, UK
Phone: +44 28 9065 7228

#297
A Wear
Category: Women's Clothing
Average price: Under £10
Address: Unit 4-5 Forestside Shopping
Centre Belfast BT8 6FX, UK
Phone: +44 28 9069 0940

#298
Keens Interiors
Category: Furniture Store
Average price: Above £46
Address: 186 Albertbridge Rd
Belfast BT5 4GS, UK
Phone: +44 28 9045 3310

#299
Park Centre
Category: Shopping Centre
Average price: £11-25
Address: Donegall Road
Belfast BT12 6HN, UK
Phone: +44 28 9032 3451

#300
Xtra Vision
Category: Videos & Games Rental
Average price: £11-25
Address: 449 Ormeau Road
Belfast BT7 3GQ, UK
Phone: +44 28 9064 0288

#301
Clements Gifts
Category: Flowers & Gifts, Jewelry
Average price: £11-25
Address: 18 Cregagh Rd
Belfast BT6 9EP, UK
Phone: +44 28 9045 1664

#302
Kiddy Junior
Category: Baby Gear & Furniture
Average price: £26-45
Address: 166a Lisburn Rd
Belfast BT9 7, UK
Phone: +44 28 9066 4550

#303
Angelo
Category: Accessories
Average price: Above £46
Address: 1a Lesley Plaza
Belfast BT9 6GN, UK
Phone: +44 28 9068 7247

#304
Carl Scarpa
Category: Shoe Store
Average price: £26-45
Address: 605 Lisburn Rd
Belfast BT9 7GS, UK
Phone: +44 28 9066 4072

#305
The Gap
Category: Fashion
Average price: £11-25
Address: Unit 1c Castle Court
Belfast BT1 1DD, UK
Phone: +44 28 9023 6444

#306
Rail News
Category: Newspapers & Magazines
Address: Great Victoria Street
Belfast BT2 7GN, UK
Phone: +44 28 9043 4001

#307
Boots Store
Category: Drugstore
Address: Great Victoria Street
Belfast BT2 7GN, UK
Phone: +44 28 9031 0530

#308
J A Rankin & Son
Category: Furniture Store
Average price: £26-45
Address: 85 Great Victoria Street
Belfast BT2 7AF, UK
Phone: +44 28 9032 4154

#309
The Third Space
Category: Art Gallery
Address: 16 Donegall Sq S
Belfast BT1 5JA, UK
Phone: +44 28 9023 7757

#310
John Ross & Co
Aka Ross's Auctions
Category: Art Gallery
Address: 37 Montgomery St
Belfast BT1 4NX, UK
Phone: +44 28 9032 5448

#311
Stephen Shaw Gallery
Category: Art Gallery
Address: 125 Great Victoria Street
Belfast BT2 7AH, UK
Phone: +44 7901 814848

#312
Thomas
Category: Jewelry
Address: 54 Upper Arthur Street
Belfast BT1 4GJ, UK
Phone: +44 28 9024 3079

#313
Quik Snaps
Category: Photography Store
Average price: £11-25
Address: 23 Shaftesbury Square
Belfast BT2 7DB, UK
Phone: +44 28 9023 0365

#314
Pronuptia
Category: Bridal
Average price: £11-25
Address: 16 Wellington Place
Belfast BT1 6GE, UK
Phone: +44 28 9032 4747

#315
Top Shop / Top Man
Category: Men's Clothing
Average price: Under £10
Address: 51 Donegall Pl
Belfast BT1 5AG, UK
Phone: +44 28 9032 3221

#316
Next Retail
Category: Fashion
Address: 40-46 Donegall Place
Belfast BT1 5BA, UK
Phone: +44 28 9034 8600

#317
Bradbury Gallery
Category: Art Gallery
Address: 1 Lyndon Court
Belfast BT1 6BT, UK
Phone: +44 28 9026 8450

#318
Nicola Russell Studio
Category: Art Gallery
Address: 37 Queen St
Belfast BT1 6EA, UK
Phone: +44 28 9031 4444

#319
Toytown
Category: Toy Store
Address: 9-15 Queen Street
Belfast BT1 6EA, UK
Phone: +44 28 9023 9399

#320
Brushstrokes
Category: Art Supplies
Address: 9-15 Queen St
Belfast BT1 6EA, UK
Phone: +44 28 9031 4326

#321
Brush Strokes
Category: Home Decor
Address: 9-15 Queen St
Belfast BT1 6EA, UK
Phone: +44 28 9031 4326

#322
Card House
Category: Cards & Stationery
Address: 5-9 Ann St
Belfast BT1 4EA, UK
Phone: +44 28 9024 5211

#323
Mace
Category: Tobacco Shop
Address: 47 Castle St
Belfast BT1 1GH, UK
Phone: +44 28 9032 5363

#324
S.D.
Category: Department Store
Average price: £26-45
Address: Bedford Street
Belfast BT2 7DF, UK
Phone: +44 28 9031 2657

#325
Red Barn Gallery
Category: Art Gallery
Address: 43b Rosemary St
Belfast BT1 1QB, UK
Phone: +44 7821 260883

#326
Innisfree Newsagents
Category: Tobacco Shop,
Newspapers & Magazines
Address: 101 Castle St
Belfast BT1 1GJ, UK
Phone: +44 28 9031 1390

#327
Snappy Snaps Franchises
Category: Photography Store
Address: 37 High Street
Belfast BT1 2AB, UK
Phone: +44 28 9032 0949

#328
Casbah Boutique
Category: Women's Clothing
Address: 33 Rosemary Street
Belfast BT1 1QB, UK
Phone: +44 28 9043 4447

#329
Lunn John H Jewellers
Category: Jewelry
Average price: Above £46
Address: Queen's Arcade
Belfast BT1 5FE, UK
Phone: +44 28 9032 9799

#330
Scenes
Category: Art Gallery
Address: 18 North Street
Belfast BT1 1LA, UK
Phone: +44 28 9024 7878

#331
Warehouse
Category: Fashion
Address: Royal Avenue
Belfast BT1 1DD, UK
Phone: +44 28 9043 9606

#332
Open Window Productions
Category: Art Gallery
Address: 25 Donegall Street
Belfast BT1 2FF, UK
Phone: +44 28 9032 9669

#333
Harper
Category: Leather Goods, Accessories
Average price: Above £46
Address: 16 Skipper Street
Belfast BT1 2DY, UK
Phone: +44 28 9024 3610

#334
Premier Record Store
Category: Music & DVDs
Address: 3-5 Smithfield
Belfast BT1 1JE, UK
Phone: +44 28 9024 0896

#335
Monsoon
Category: Women's Clothing
Address: Victoria Sq
Belfast BT1 4QG, UK
Phone: +44 28 9032 2547

#336
Reiss
Category: Fashion
Address: Victoria Sq
Belfast BT1 4QG, UK
Phone: +44 28 9032 3695

#337
The MAC
Category: Art Gallery, Cultural Center
Address: 10 Exchange Street West
Belfast BT1 2NJ, UK
Phone: +44 28 9023 5053

#338
F & J Kennedy
Category: Shopping Centre
Address: 35 Gresham Street
Belfast BT1 1JL, UK
Phone: +44 28 9032 3535

#339
The Body Jewellery Shop
Category: Jewelry
Average price: £26-45
Address: 17 Fountain Street
Belfast BT1 2JZ, UK
Phone: +44 28 9023 8537

#340
MK One
Category: Fashion
Average price: Under £10
Address: Unit 60 Castle Court
Belfast BT1 1DD, UK
Phone: +44 28 9023 3052

#341
Boxing Equipment
Category: Sporting Goods
Average price: £11-25
Address: Smithfield Market
Belfast BT1 1JQ, UK
Phone: +44 7706 512571

#342
Living Oasis
Category: Music & DVDs, Bookstore
Average price: £11-25
Address: Fisherwick Pl
Belfast BT1 6DW, UK
Phone: +44 28 9032 1323

#343
Bargain World
Category: Hardware Store
Average price: Under £10
Address: 171 Shankill Rd
Belfast BT13 1, UK
Phone: +44 28 9058 2299

#344
Egg I.T.
Category: Office Equipment, Computers
Average price: £11-25
Address: 275 Woodstock Road
Belfast BT6 8PR, UK
Phone: +44 28 9020 1200

#345
Oriel Pharmacy
Category: Drugstore
Average price: £11-25
Address: 363 Ormeau Road
Belfast BT7 3GP, UK
Phone: +44 28 9049 1325

#346
Gormleys Fine Art
Category: Art Gallery
Average price: £26-45
Address: 251 Lisburn Road
Belfast BT9 7EN, UK
Phone: +44 28 9066 3313

#347
Crown Decorating Centre
Category: Home Decor
Average price: £11-25
Address: 374 Albertbridge Rd
Belfast BT5 4PY, UK
Phone: +44 28 9045 7928

#348
Quilters Quest
Category: Fabric Store
Average price: £11-25
Address: 361 Woodstock Road
Belfast BT6 8PU, UK
Phone: +44 28 9045 4745

#349
Eastend Video 2
Category: Videos & Games Rental
Average price: Under £10
Address: 414 Woodstock Road
Belfast BT6 9DQ, UK
Phone: +44 28 9046 9939

#350
Flowers Of Elegance
Category: Florist
Average price: Under £10
Address: Castlereagh Road
Belfast BT5 5FL, UK
Phone: +44 28 9045 4448

#351
Dorothy Perkins
Category: Women's Clothing
Average price: £26-45
Address: Boucher Rd
Belfast BT12 6HR, UK
Phone: +44 28 9066 8856

#352
New Look
Category: Women's Clothing,
Men's Clothing
Average price: £11-25
Address: Boucher Retail Park Boucher
Crescent Belfast BT12 6HU, UK
Phone: +44 28 9068 8640

#353
James Mcdonagh
Category: Drugstore
Average price: £11-25
Address: 233-235 Falls Road
Belfast BT12 6FB, UK
Phone: +44 28 9032 5046

#354
Action Cancer
Category: Thrift Store
Average price: Under £10
Address: 455 Ormeau Rd
Belfast BT7 2, UK
Phone: +44 28 9069 2351

#355
Jean's Wool Shop
Category: Knitting Supplies
Average price: Under £10
Address: 26 Cregagh Rd
Belfast BT6 9EQ, UK
Phone: +44 28 9045 6388

#356
Boot's
Category: Drugstore
Average price: £11-25
Address: 77 Cregagh Rd
Belfast BT6 8PY, UK
Phone: +44 28 9045 7606

#357
Wyse Byse
Category: Department Store
Average price: Under £10
Address: 387-389 Newtownards Road
Belfast BT4 1AJ, UK
Phone: +44 28 9045 5680

#358
Peel Fashion Store
Category: Women's Clothing
Average price: Above £46
Address: 107 Bloomfield Avenue
Belfast BT5 5AB, UK
Phone: +44 28 9045 2665

#359
The Alexandra
Category: Florist
Average price: £11-25
Address: 88 York Road
Belfast BT15 3HF, UK
Phone: +44 28 9035 1184

#360
Arches House of Lights
Category: Home & Garden
Average price: £11-25
Address: 16-22 Upper Newtownards Road
Belfast BT4 3EL, UK
Phone: +44 28 9065 7415

#361
Rite Price Carpet & Furniture
Category: Furniture Store
Average price: £11-25
Address: 95-111 York Road
Belfast BT15 3GY, UK
Phone: +44 28 9075 2777

#362
Lyle's Floorcoverings
Category: Home & Garden
Average price: £26-45
Address: 384-386 Lisburn Road
Belfast BT9 6GN, UK
Phone: +44 28 9066 5082

#363
JD Sports
Category: Sporting Goods
Average price: £11-25
Address: 14 Donegall Pl
Belfast BT1 5BA, UK
Phone: +44 28 9024 5988

#364
Shoe Zone
Category: Shoe Store
Average price: Under £10
Address: 35-37 Castle St
Belfast BT1 1PS, UK
Phone: +44 28 9031 4053

#365
Kolor Master Ireland
Category: Shopping, Printing Services
Average price: Under £10
Address: 535e Falls Rd
Belfast BT11 9AA, UK
Phone: +44 28 9061 6552

#366
AllSaints
Category: Fashion
Average price: £26-45
Address: LG04 Victoria Sq
Belfast BT1 4QB, UK
Phone: +44 4428 9031 6140

#367
Rituals
Category: Cosmetics & Beauty Supply,
Flowers & Gifts
Average price: £26-45
Address: Victoria Sq
Belfast BT1 4QG, UK
Phone: +44 28 9032 0489

#368
Belmont Pharmacy
Category: Drugstore
Average price: Under £10
Address: 50 Belmont Road
Belfast BT4 2AN, UK
Phone: +44 28 9047 1629

#369
Dawsons Newsagency
Category: Newspapers & Magazines
Average price: Under £10
Address: 52 Belmont Rd
Belfast BT4 2AN, UK
Phone: +44 28 9047 1087

#370
Priceless Shoes
Category: Shoe Store
Average price: Under £10
Address: Kennedy Centre 564-568 Falls
Road Belfast BT11 9AE, UK
Phone: +44 28 9062 8340

#371
The Bureau
Category: Fashion
Average price: Above £46
Address: 46-50 Howard St
Belfast BT1 6PG, UK
Phone: +44 28 9032 6100

#372
Brazil
Category: Women's Clothing
Average price: £26-45
Address: 41 Bradbury Place
Belfast BT7 1RR, UK
Phone: +44 28 9032 5504

#373
Xtra Vision
Category: Videos & Games Rental
Average price: Under £10
Address: 1 Kennedy Centre
Belfast BT11 9AE, UK
Phone: +44 28 9062 5811

#374
HMV
Category: Music & DVDs
Average price: £11-25
Address: Forestside Shopping Centre
Newtownbreda
Belfast BT8 6FX, UK
Phone: +44 843 221 0117

#375
Canvas
Category: Framing
Average price: £26-45
Address: 66 Stranmillis Rd
Belfast BT9 5AD, UK
Phone: +44 28 9022 2727

#376
Botanic Pharmacy
Category: Drugstore
Average price: £11-25
Address: 98 Botanic Avenue
Belfast BT7 1JR, UK
Phone: +44 28 9032 5509

#377
Whinstone Agencies
Category: Appliances
Average price: £11-25
Address: 5 D C Enterprise Centre
Belfast BT11 9AP, UK
Phone: +44 28 9030 1997

#378
Best Sellers
Category: Grocery, Discount Store
Average price: Under £10
Address: 12 North St
Belfast BT1 1LA, UK
Phone: +44 28 9031 5395

#379
Kurt Geiger
Category: Shopping
Average price: Above £46
Address: Victoria Sq
Belfast BT1 4QG, UK
Phone: +44 28 9024 6024

#380
Fullarton Pharmacy
Category: Drugstore
Average price: Under £10
Address: Oxford St
Belfast BT1 3NQ, UK
Phone: +44 28 9023 3101

#381
Lenas Newsagents
Category: Newspapers & Magazines
Average price: Under £10
Address: 9 Twin Spires Centre
Belfast BT13 2JF, UK
Phone: +44 28 9024 4853

#382
Calvin Klein Underwear
Category: Women's Clothing,
Men's Clothing, Lingerie
Average price: £26-45
Address: 1 Victoria Sqaure
Belfast BT1 4QG, UK
Phone: +44 28 9033 2476

#383
Gosh Design
Category: Home & Garden
Average price: Above £46
Address: 81-99 York Street
Belfast BT15 1AB, UK
Phone: +44 28 9023 9037

#384
The Wingrove
Category: Newspapers & Magazines
Average price: Under £10
Address: 368 Upper Newtownards Road
Belfast BT4 3EX, UK
Phone: +44 28 9047 1127

#385
Stormont Antiques
Category: Antiques, Jewelry
Average price: £11-25
Address: 2c Sandown Road
Belfast BT5 6GY, UK
Phone: +44 28 9047 2586

#386
Eakin Gallery
Category: Art Gallery
Average price: £26-45
Address: 237 Lisburn Road
Belfast BT9 7EN, UK
Phone: +44 28 9066 8522

#387
Sandown Pharmacy
Category: Drugstore
Average price: Under £10
Address: 390 Upper Newtownards Rd
Belfast BT4 3EY, UK
Phone: +44 28 9065 5166

#388
JD Sports
Category: Sporting Goods
Average price: £11-25
Address: Boucher Retail Park Boucher
Crescent Belfast BT12 6HU, UK
Phone: +44 28 9068 7823

#389
Splash
Category: Shoe Store
Average price: £26-45
Address: 106 Bloomfield Ave
Belfast BT5 5AB, UK
Phone: +44 28 9045 7226

#390
Funky Bedrooms
Category: Home Decor,
Baby Gear & Furniture
Average price: £26-45
Address: Bloomfield Avenue
Belfast BT5 5, UK
Phone: +44 28 9045 4959

#391
Paul Cooper
Category: Drugstore
Average price: £11-25
Address: 155 Andersonstown Road
Belfast BT11 9EA, UK
Phone: +44 28 9060 2500

#392
Jourdan
Category: Women's Clothing
Average price: £26-45
Address: 733 Lisburn Road
Belfast BT9 7GU, UK
Phone: +44 28 9068 2944

#393
Spires Mall
Category: Shopping Center
Average price: £11-25
Address: Church House
Belfast BT1 6DW, UK
Phone: +44 28 9032 2284

#394
Hollister
Category: Women's Clothing,
Men's Clothing, Accessories
Average price: £26-45
Address: 1 Victoria Sq
Belfast BT1 4QG, UK
Phone: +44 28 9043 8154

#395
Hatch Bros
Category: Hardware Store
Average price: £11-25
Address: 147 Upper Lisburn Road
Belfast BT10 0LH, UK
Phone: +44 28 9061 4526

#396
Fleuriste Florist
Category: Florist
Average price: £11-25
Address: 124 Upper Lisburn Road
Belfast BT10 0BD, UK
Phone: +44 28 9060 1616

#397
The Card Crew
Category: Cards & Stationery
Average price: £11-25
Address: 4 Castlehill Farm
Belfast BT5 7GU, UK
Phone: +44 7749 198022

#398
Rip Off
Category: Tobacco Shop, Accessories
Average price: £11-25
Address: 32 Donegall St
Belfast BT2 7, UK
Phone: +44 28 9043 4849

#399
Picture Gallery
Category: Art Gallery
Average price: £11-25
Address: 35 Queen St
Belfast BT1 6EA, UK
Phone: +44 28 9024 2885

#400
Zamba Shoe Shop
Category: Shoe Store
Average price: £26-45
Address: 8 Kings Square
Belfast BT5 7EA, UK
Phone: +44 28 9079 7908

#401
Price Is Right
Category: Flowers & Gifts
Average price: Under £10
Address: 29 Botanic Avenue
Belfast BT7 1JG, UK
Phone: +44 28 9032 5313

#402
Johnathan Hall
Category: Eyewear & Opticians
Average price: £11-25
Address: 7 Kings Square
Belfast BT5 7EA, UK
Phone: +44 28 9070 5787

#403
Bells Store
Category: Shopping
Average price: Under £10
Address: 4 Kings Square
Belfast BT5 7EA, UK
Phone: +44 28 9079 3701

#404
Dunelm Mill
Category: Home Decor
Average price: Under £10
Address: Shane Retail Park Boucher Road
Belfast BT12 6HR, UK
Phone: +44 28 9066 7250

#405
Andrew Watson Menswear
Category: Men's Clothing
Average price: Above £46
Address: 11 Upper Queen Street
Belfast BT1 6FB, UK
Phone: +44 28 9024 3412

#406
Remarkable Flowers
Category: Florist
Average price: Under £10
Address: 147 Holywood Road
Belfast BT4 3BE, UK
Phone: +44 7714 941374

#407
7 Camicie Roma
Category: Men's Clothing
Average price: £26-45
Address: Victoria Sq
Belfast BT1 4, UK
Phone: +44 28 9024 9640

#408
Rio & Brazil
Category: Fashion
Average price: £26-45
Address: 43 Bradbury Pl
Belfast BT7 1RR, UK
Phone: +44 28 9032 5504

#409
All Saints Retail
Category: Fashion
Average price: £11-25
Address: 36-40 Victoria Square
Belfast BT1 4QB, UK
Phone: +44 28 9031 6140

#410
Hanna & Browne Home Gifts
Category: Flowers & Gifts
Average price: £11-25
Address: 21 Fountain St
Belfast BT1 5EA, UK
Phone: +44 28 9032 5775

#411
The Bridge News
Category: Newspapers & Magazines
Average price: Under £10
Address: 11 Bridge Street
Belfast BT1 1LT, UK
Phone: +44 28 9023 2625

#412
Irwin's Medical Hall
Category: Drugstore
Average price: Under £10
Address: 167 Kingsway
Belfast BT17 9RY, UK
Phone: +44 28 9061 8022

#413
Kingsway Pharmacy
Category: Drugstore
Average price: Under £10
Address: 175 Kingsway
Belfast BT17 9RY, UK
Phone: +44 28 9030 1638

#414
The Carphone Warehouse
Category: Mobile Phones
Average price: £11-25
Address: Castle Court
Belfast BT1 1DD, UK
Phone: +44 28 9024 3614

#415
D2
Category: Fashion
Average price: £11-25
Address: Castle Ct
Belfast BT1 1DD, UK
Phone: +44 28 9023 3546

#416
River Island Clothing Co
Category: Fashion
Average price: £26-45
Address: 1 Boucher Crescent
Belfast BT12 6HU, UK
Phone: +44 28 9066 7499

#417
Dead On
Category: Women's Clothing
Average price: £11-25
Address: Unit 41 CastleCourt
Belfast BT1 1DD, UK
Phone: +44 28 9033 2392

#418
First Class
Category: Fashion
Average price: £11-25
Address: 54 Bloomfield Avenue
Belfast BT5 5AD, UK
Phone: +44 28 9045 3370

#419
Reid Furniture
Category: Furniture Store
Average price: £11-25
Address: Boucher Road
Belfast BT12 6UA, UK
Phone: +44 28 9038 2109

#420
Tom Browne
Category: Newspapers & Magazines
Average price: Under £10
Address: 1 Dublin Road
Belfast BT2 7HB, UK
Phone: +44 28 9032 0329

#421
Archives Antique Dealers
Category: Antiques
Average price: £11-25
Address: 88 Donegall Passage
Belfast BT7 1BX, UK
Phone: +44 28 9023 2383

#422
Oakland Antiques
Category: Antiques
Average price: £26-45
Address: 135-137 Donegall Passage
Belfast BT7 1DS, UK
Phone: +44 28 9023 0176

#423
Parklane Jewellers
Category: Jewelry
Average price: £11-25
Address: 10 Botanic Ave
Belfast BT7 1JQ, UK
Phone: +44 28 9023 1626

#424
Vodafone
Category: Mobile Phones
Average price: £11-25
Address: 22 Donegall Pl
Belfast BT1 5BA, UK
Phone: +44 28 9027 8611

#425
East
Category: Fashion
Average price: £11-25
Address: 8 Castle Place
Belfast BT1 1GB, UK
Phone: +44 28 9032 4880

#426
Selection Box
Category: Discount Store
Average price: Under £10
Address: 72-80 Castle St
Belfast BT1 1HD, UK
Phone: +44 28 9031 5829

#427
The Watch Shop
Category: Accessories
Average price: £26-45
Address: Queens Arcade
Belfast BT1, UK
Phone: +44 28 9033 2250

#428
Royal Ulster Rifles Museum
Category: Museum, Art Gallery
Average price: Under £10
Address: 5 Waring Street
Belfast BT1 2EW, UK
Phone: +44 28 9023 2086

#429
The Good Book Shop
Category: Bookstore
Average price: £11-25
Address: 61-67 Donegall Street
Belfast BT1 2QH, UK
Phone: +44 28 9082 8890

#430
Charles Gilmore Fine Art
Category: Art Gallery
Average price: £26-45
Address: 1 Lanyon Quay
Belfast BT1 3LG, UK
Phone: +44 28 9031 1666

#431
Phoenix Gallery
Category: Art Gallery
Average price: £11-25
Address: Great Victoria St
Belfast BT2 7HR, UK
Phone: +44 28 9024 1919

#432
Expectations
Category: Eyewear & Opticians
Average price: £26-45
Address: 131 Stranmillis Road
Belfast BT9 5AJ, UK
Phone: +44 28 9066 2897

#433
Urban Planting by Reids
Category: Florist
Average price: £26-45
Address: 154-156 Lisburn Rd
Belfast BT9 6AJ, UK
Phone: +44 28 9002 0698

#434
James Harden
Category: Furniture Store
Average price: £11-25
Address: 85 Falls Road
Belfast BT12 4PE, UK
Phone: +44 28 9029 0700

#435
James Harden 2
Category: Furniture Store
Average price: £11-25
Address: 85 Falls Road
Belfast BT12 4PE, UK
Phone: +44 28 9023 4824

#436
Mcpeakes Florist
Category: Florist
Average price: £11-25
Address: 111 Falls Road
Belfast BT12 6AA, UK
Phone: +44 28 9024 0820

#437
S Mcpeake Paints
Category: Hardware Store
Average price: £11-25
Address: 111 Falls Road
Belfast BT12 6AA, UK
Phone: +44 28 9024 9643

#438
Ornamental Garden
Category: Landscaping,
Nurseries & Gardening
Average price: £11-25
Address: 1-3 Pim St
Belfast BT15 2DN, UK
Phone: +44 7971 641335

#439
Asda Living
Category: Home Decor
Average price: £11-25
Address: 100-150 York St
Belfast BT15 1WA, UK
Phone: +44 28 9035 7770

#440
Kitsons Shoes
Category: Shoe Store
Average price: Under £10
Address: 249 Shankill Road
Belfast BT13 1FR, UK
Phone: +44 28 9023 4805

#441
Star Lighting
Category: Home & Garden
Average price: £11-25
Address: 259 Shankill Road
Belfast BT13 1FR, UK
Phone: +44 28 9059 6111

#442
Barr & Co
Category: Shoe Store
Average price: Under £10
Address: 368-370 Woodstock Road
Belfast BT6 9DQ, UK
Phone: +44 28 9045 8778

#443
Crysalis
Category: Shopping
Average price: Under £10
Address: 375 Woodstock Rd
Belfast BT6 8PU, UK
Phone: +44 28 9073 9608

#444
Quinns
Category: Flowers & Gifts
Average price: £11-25
Address: 285-287 Shankill Road
Belfast BT13 1FT, UK
Phone: +44 28 9027 8895

#445
North Queen Street Pharmacy
Category: Drugstore
Average price: Under £10
Address: 142 North Queen Street
Belfast BT15 1HQ, UK
Phone: +44 28 9074 6109

#446
Ohares Hardware Store
Category: Hardware Store
Average price: £11-25
Address: 223 Falls Road
Belfast BT12 6FB, UK
Phone: +44 28 9032 2318

#447
The Cultúrlann
Category: Art Gallery
Average price: £11-25
Address: 216 Falls Rd
Belfast BT12 6AH, UK
Phone: +44 28 9096 4180

#448
Shankill Furnishings
Category: Furniture Store
Average price: £11-25
Address: 391 Shankill Road
Belfast BT13 3AF, UK
Phone: +44 28 9024 7885

#449
Caldwell
Category: Art Gallery
Average price: £26-45
Address: 429-431 Lisburn Road
Belfast BT9 7EY, UK
Phone: +44 28 9066 1890

#450
War On Want
Category: Thrift Store
Average price: £11-25
Address: 63 Cregagh Rd
Belfast BT6 8PX, UK
Phone: +44 28 9045 4061

#451
Flowers Are Us
Category: Florist
Average price: £11-25
Address: 257 Falls Road
Belfast BT12 6FB, UK
Phone: +44 28 9033 0018

#452
Loopland Pharmacy
Category: Drugstore
Average price: £11-25
Address: 253 Castlereagh Rd
Belfast BT5 5FL, UK
Phone: +44 28 9045 7629

#453
Maureen's Florist
Category: Florist
Average price: £11-25
Address: 467 Falls Road
Belfast BT12 6DD, UK
Phone: +44 28 9032 2860

#454
White Bicycle
Category: Women's Clothing
Average price: £26-45
Address: 50 Bloomfield Avenue
Belfast BT5 5AD, UK
Phone: +44 28 9045 7719

#455
T A Maguire
Category: Drugstore
Average price: £11-25
Address: 505 Falls Road
Belfast BT12 6DE, UK
Phone: +44 28 9032 7140

#456
Ltd2
Category: Men's Clothing,
Women's Clothing
Average price: £26-45
Address: 9 Upper Queen Street
Belfast BT1 6FB, UK
Phone: +44 28 9031 5000

#457
BHS
Category: Department Store
Average price: £11-25
Address: 24-26 Castle Pl
Belfast BT1 1GB, UK
Phone: +44 28 9024 3068

#458
Cotswold
Category: Hobby Shop
Average price: £26-45
Address: Boucher Crescent
Belfast BT12 6HU, UK
Phone: +44 28 9066 5003

#459
Barratt Shoes
Category: Shoe Store
Average price: Under £10
Address: Unit 42 Connswater Shopping
Centre Belfast BT5 5LP, UK
Phone: +44 28 9045 8255

#460
Grampian Furniture
Category: Furniture Store
Average price: £11-25
Address: 20-22 Holywood Road
Belfast BT4 1NT, UK
Phone: +44 28 9065 5227

#461
Biento Madame
Category: Bridal
Average price: £11-25
Address: 115-119 Royal Avenue
Belfast BT1 1FF, UK
Phone: +44 28 9023 3247

#462
Maplin Electronics
Category: Electronics
Average price: £11-25
Address: 55 Boucher Rd
Belfast BT12 6HR, UK
Phone: +44 843 227 7350

#463
Lakeland
Category: Kitchen & Bath
Average price: £26-45
Address: Unit 3 Balmoral Plaza
Belfast BT12 6HR, UK
Phone: +44 28 9068 3229

#464
Moda
Category: Shoe Store
Average price: £26-45
Address: 667 Lisburn Road
Belfast BT9 7GT, UK
Phone: +44 28 9066 5560

#465
Claire's Accessories
Category: Accessories
Average price: Under £10
Address: Castle Court
Belfast BT1 1SU, UK
Phone: +44 28 9024 6911

#466
Glen Florist & Limousine
Category: Florist
Average price: £11-25
Address: 13 Glen Road
Belfast BT11 8BA, UK
Phone: +44 28 9060 1999

#467
Monty At The Arches
Category: Shoe Store
Average price: £11-25
Address: 31 Belmont Road
Belfast BT4 2AA, UK
Phone: +44 28 9067 3447

#468
Sainsbury's
Category: Department Store, Grocery
Average price: £26-45
Address: 564-568 Falls Rd
Belfast BT12 6, UK
Phone: +44 28 9061 6386

#469
Copycats
Category: Printing Services,
Cards & Stationery, Framing
Average price: Under £10
Address: 537 Antrim Road
Belfast BT15 3BU, UK
Phone: +44 28 9077 6457

#470
Asda
Category: Department Store, Grocery
Average price: £11-25
Address: Westwood Centre Kennedy Way
Belfast BT11 9BQ, UK
Phone: +44 28 9060 3644

#471
Monagh Fashions & Sports
Category: Sports Wear
Average price: £11-25
Address: Unit 9 Norglen Gardens
Belfast BT11 8EL, UK
Phone: +44 28 9060 0851

#472
Fortwilliam Garden Centre
Category: Nurseries & Gardening
Average price: Under £10
Address: 575 Antrim Road
Belfast BT15 3BU, UK
Phone: +44 28 9077 1013

#473
Doherty's Pharmacy
Category: Drugstore
Average price: £11-25
Address: 115 Andersonstown Road
Belfast BT11 9BT, UK
Phone: +44 28 9061 3832

#474
Rent Tel Television Service
Category: Electronics
Average price: £11-25
Address: 150 Andersonstown Road
Belfast BT11 9BY, UK
Phone: +44 28 9060 4433

#475
Flower Bay
Category: Florist
Average price: Under £10
Address: 78 Andersonstown Road
Belfast BT11 9AN, UK
Phone: +44 28 9061 1977

#476
Papermill Wallpapers
Category: Home Decor
Average price: £11-25
Address: 170 Andersonstown Road
Belfast BT11 9BZ, UK
Phone: +44 28 9030 1376

#477
Noel Grimley Electrics
Category: Appliances
Average price: £11-25
Address: 176 Andersonstown Road
Belfast BT11 9BZ, UK
Phone: +44 28 9061 5327

#478
Pulse Clothing
Category: Men's Clothing,
Women's Clothing
Average price: Above £46
Address: 17 Wellington Pl
Belfast BT1 4GD, UK
Phone: +44 28 9033 3595

#479
Wee Carnaby Centre
Category: Tobacco Shop, Fashion
Average price: £11-25
Address: Units 48 - 50 InShop
Belfast BT1 2JZ, UK
Phone: +44 28 9080 5282

#480
Laura Ashley
Category: Home Decor
Average price: £26-45
Address: Boucher Retail Park Boucher
Crescent Belfast BT12 6HU, UK
Phone: +44 871 223 1561

#481
The Carphone Warehouse
Category: Mobile Phones
Average price: Under £10
Address: East Bread Street
Belfast BT5 5AP, UK
Phone: +44 870 168 2191

#482
DFS Furniture Company
Category: Furniture Store
Average price: £11-25
Address: 49 Boucher Road
Belfast BT12 6HR, UK
Phone: +44 28 9068 7472

#483
The Potting Shed
Category: Florist
Average price: Under £10
Address: 6 Kings Square
Belfast BT5 7EA, UK
Phone: +44 28 9079 9414

#484
Penelope Flowers
Category: Florist
Average price: £26-45
Address: Kings Square
Belfast BT5 7BP, UK
Phone: +44 28 9079 3791

#485
Little Petal
Category: Florist, Coffee & Tea
Average price: Under £10
Address: 121 Gilnahirk Road
Belfast BT5 7QL, UK
Phone: +44 28 9079 0748

#486
Hillmount Nursery Centre
Category: Nurseries & Gardening
Average price: £11-25
Address: 56-58 Upper Braniel Road
Belfast BT5 7TX, UK
Phone: +44 28 9044 8213

#487
Cook's Day Today
Category: Newspapers & Magazines
Average price: £11-25
Address: 119 Ormeau Road
Belfast BT7 1SH, UK
Phone: +44 28 9024 9229

#488
Pound Town
Category: Flowers & Gifts
Average price: Under £10
Address: 116 Andersonstown Road
Belfast BT11 9BX, UK
Phone: +44 28 9030 0810

#489
HMV
Category: Music & DVDs
Average price: £11-25
Address: Boucher Rd
Belfast BT12 6HU, UK
Phone: +44 843 221 0118

#490
Cregagh Video Club
Category: Videos & Games Rental
Average price: Under £10
Address: 46 Cregagh Rd
Belfast BT6 9EQ, UK
Phone: +44 28 9045 1658

#491
Semi-Chem
Category: Drugstore
Average price: Under £10
Address: 37 Park Centre
Belfast BT12 6HN, UK
Phone: +44 28 9023 1123

#492
Mckenzie's Pharmacy
Category: Drugstore
Average price: £11-25
Address: 479 Falls Road
Belfast BT12 6DE, UK
Phone: +44 28 9032 2152

#493
Langford Shoes
Category: Shoe Store
Average price: Under £10
Address: 10 Lower North Street
Belfast BT1 1LA, UK
Phone: +44 28 9032 7553

#494
Frame Academy
Category: Framing
Average price: £11-25
Address: 168 Cavehill Road
Belfast BT15 5EX, UK
Phone: +44 28 9072 9433

#495
Wolseys Tackle Shop
Category: Sporting Goods
Average price: £11-25
Address: 60 Upper Newtownards Road
Belfast BT4 3EN, UK
Phone: +44 28 9047 1131

#496
**The Alteration Boutique
By Ingrid**
Category: Sewing & Alterations, Bridal
Average price: Above £46
Address: 11 Upper Queen Street
Belfast BT1 6FB, UK
Phone: +44 28 9031 3847

#497
Poundland
Category: Discount Store
Average price: Under £10
Address: Bloomfield Ave
Belfast BT5 5DL, UK
Phone: +44 28 9045 3113

#498
Yoke Clothing
Category: Men's Clothing,
Women's Clothing
Average price: £26-45
Address: 5 Wellington Buildings
Belfast BT1 6HT, UK
Phone: +44 28 9023 6900

#499
Vodafone Retail
Category: Shopping Center
Average price: £11-25
Address: Royal Avenue
Belfast BT1 1DD, UK
Phone: +44 28 9023 4591

#500
Work Rest Play Interiors
Category: Furniture Store
Average price: £11-25
Address: 70-74 Donegall Street
Belfast BT1 2GU, UK
Phone: +44 28 9031 4303

TOP 500 RESTAURANTS

Recommended by Locals & Trevelers

(From #1 to #500)

#1
The Merchant Hotel
Cuisines: Hotel, European
Average price: Above £46
Address: 35 - 39 Waring Street
Belfast BT1 2DY, UK
Phone: +44 28 9023 4888

#2
Mourne Seafood Bar
Cuisines: Seafood
Average price: £11-25
Address: 34-36 Bank Street
Belfast BT1 1HL, UK
Phone: +44 28 9024 8544

#3
Boojum
Cuisines: Mexican
Average price: Under £10
Address: 73 Botanic Avenue
Belfast BT7 1JL, UK
Phone: +44 28 9031 5334

#4
Arcadia
Cuisines: Delis, Specialty Food
Average price: £11-25
Address: 378 Lisburn Road
Belfast BT9 6GL, UK
Phone: +44 28 9038 1779

#5
Made In Belfast
Cuisines: Irish, British, European
Average price: £11-25
Address: Wellington St
Belfast BT1 6ET, UK
Phone: +44 28 9024 6712

#6
Muriel's
Cuisines: Lounge, European
Average price: £11-25
Address: 12-14 Church Lane
Belfast BT1 4QN, UK
Phone: +44 28 9033 2445

#7
Spaniard
Cuisines: Pub, GastroPub
Average price: £26-45
Address: 3 Skipper Street
Belfast BT1 2DZ, UK
Phone: +44 28 9023 2448

#8
La Boca
Cuisines: Argentine
Average price: £11-25
Address: Unit 6 Fountain Street
Belfast BT1 5ED, UK
Phone: +44 28 9032 3087

#9
Villa Italia
Cuisines: Italian, Pizza
Average price: £11-25
Address: 37-41 University Road
Belfast BT7 1ND, UK
Phone: +44 28 9032 8356

#10
White's Tavern
Cuisines: Pub, GastroPub
Average price: £11-25
Address: 2-4 Winecellar Entry
Belfast BT1 1QN, UK
Phone: +44 28 9024 3080

#11
Rocket & Relish Gourmet Burger
Cuisines: Burgers
Average price: Under £10
Address: 479-481 Lisburn Road
Belfast BT9 7GU, UK
Phone: +44 28 9066 5655

#12
Olio
Cuisines: European
Average price: £11-25
Address: 17 Brunswick Street
Belfast BT2 7GE, UK
Phone: +44 28 9024 0239

#13
Doorsteps
Cuisines: Coffee & Tea,
Sandwiches, Delicatessen
Average price: Under £10
Address: 455-457 Lisburn Road
Belfast BT9 7EY, UK
Phone: +44 28 9068 1645

#14
Zen Japenese Restuarant
Cuisines: Japanese, Sushi Bar
Average price: £26-45
Address: 55-59 Adelaide Street
Belfast BT2 8FE, UK
Phone: +44 28 9023 2244

#15
The Ginger Bistro
Cuisines: European
Average price: £26-45
Address: 7-8 Hope Street
Belfast BT12 5EE, UK
Phone: +44 28 9024 4421

#16
Long's Restaurant
Cuisines: Seafood, Fish & Chips
Average price: Under £10
Address: 39 Athol Street
Belfast BT12 4GX, UK
Phone: +44 28 9032 1848

#17
The Yellow Door Deli
Cuisines: Delis, Caterers
Average price: Under £10
Address: 427 Lisburn Road
Belfast BT9 7EY, UK
Phone: +44 28 9038 1961

#18
Tony Roma's
Cuisines: American
Average price: £26-45
Address: 37 University Road
Belfast BT7 1ND, UK
Phone: +44 28 9032 6777

#19
Yum
Cuisines: European, Asian Fusion
Average price: £11-25
Address: 157 Stranmillis Road
Belfast BT9 5AJ, UK
Phone: +44 28 9066 8020

#20
The Sphinx
Cuisines: Fast Food
Average price: Under £10
Address: 74 Stranmillis Road
Belfast BT9 5AD, UK
Phone: +44 28 9068 1881

#21
Lunches To Go
Cuisines: Fast Food, Sandwiches
Average price: Under £10
Address: 8 Church Lane
Belfast BT1 4QN, UK
Phone: +44 28 9033 2300

#22
Apartment
Cuisines: Pub, European, Lounge
Average price: £11-25
Address: 2 Donegall Square West
Belfast BT1 6JA, UK
Phone: +44 28 9050 9777

#23
Morning Star
Cuisines: Pub, Irish
Average price: £11-25
Address: Pottinger's Entry
Belfast BT1 4DU, UK
Phone: +44 28 9032 9310

#24
West
Cuisines: Fast Food,
Breakfast & Brunch, Sandwiches
Average price: £11-25
Address: 3 Castle Street
Belfast BT1 1HB, UK
Phone: +44 28 9032 5649

#25
Garrick Bar
Cuisines: Pub, Lounge, GastroPub
Average price: £11-25
Address: 29 Chichester Street
Belfast BT1 4JB, UK
Phone: +44 28 9032 1984

#26
L'Etoile Restaurant
Cuisines: French
Average price: £11-25
Address: 407 Ormeau Road
Belfast BT7 3GP, UK
Phone: +44 28 9020 1300

#27
Ryan's Bar & Grill
Cuisines: Bar, British
Average price: £11-25
Address: 116-118 Lisburn Road
Belfast BT9 6AH, UK
Phone: +44 28 9050 9850

#28
Barking Dog Restaurant
Cuisines: European, British, Wine Bar
Average price: £11-25
Address: 33-35 Malone Road
Belfast BT9 6RU, UK
Phone: +44 28 9066 1885

#29
Sakura
Cuisines: Japanese, Sushi Bar
Average price: £11-25
Address: 82 Botanic Avenue
Belfast BT7 1JR, UK
Phone: +44 28 9043 9590

#30
Maggie Mays
Cuisines: Coffee & Tea, Burgers,
Breakfast & Brunch
Average price: Under £10
Address: 50 Botanic Avenue
Belfast BT7 1JR, UK
Phone: +44 28 9032 2662

#31
**The Grill Room and Bar
at Ten Square Hotel**
Cuisines: European, Steakhouses
Average price: £26-45
Address: 10 Donegall Square South
Belfast BT1 5JD, UK
Phone: +44 28 9024 1001

#32
Grapevine
Cuisines: Cajun/Creole, European
Average price: Under £10
Address: 5 Pottingers Entry
Belfast BT1 4DT, UK
Phone: +44 28 9023 8182

#33
Hooligan
Cuisines: European, Irish
Average price: £26-45
Address: 24 Talbot Street
Belfast BT1 2LD, UK
Phone: +44 28 9024 4107

#34
Lolita
Cuisines: Indian
Average price: £26-45
Address: 66 Stranmillis Road
Belfast BT9 5AD, UK
Phone: +44 28 9066 8087

#35
The Foo Kin Noodle Bar
Cuisines: Chinese
Average price: Under £10
Address: 38 Bradbury Place
Belfast BT7 1RS, UK
Phone: +44 28 9023 2889

#36
Bastille
Cuisines: French
Average price: £11-25
Address: 180-182 Lisburn Road
Belfast BT9 6AL, UK
Phone: +44 28 9066 7500

#37
Rhubarb
Cuisines: European
Average price: Under £10
Address: 2 Little Victoria Street
Belfast BT2 7JH, UK
Phone: +44 28 9020 0158

#38
Bishops
Cuisines: Fish & Chips
Average price: Under £10
Address: 30-34 Bradbury Place
Belfast BT7 1RS, UK
Phone: +44 28 9043 9070

#39
Tedfords
Cuisines: Seafood
Average price: £11-25
Address: 5 Donegall Quay
Belfast BT1 3EA, UK
Phone: +44 28 9043 4000

#40
House of Zen
Cuisines: Asian Fusion, Chinese
Average price: £11-25
Address: St Annes Square
Belfast BT9 6AG, UK
Phone: +44 28 9068 7318

#41
Molly's Yard
Cuisines: Irish, Pub
Average price: £26-45
Address: 1 College Green Mews
Belfast BT7 1LW, UK
Phone: +44 28 9032 2600

#42
Ginger Tree
Cuisines: Chinese, Japanese
Average price: £11-25
Address: 23 Donegall Passage
Belfast BT7 1DQ, UK
Phone: +44 28 9032 7151

#43
Pizza Express
Cuisines: Pizza, Italian
Average price: £11-25
Address: 25 Bedford Street
Belfast BT2 7EJ, UK
Phone: +44 28 9032 9050

#44
Lee Garden
Cuisines: Chinese
Average price: £11-25
Address: 14-18 Botanic Avenue
Belfast BT7 1JQ, UK
Phone: +44 28 9027 8882

#45
Beatrice Kennedy
Cuisines: American, Desserts
Average price: £26-45
Address: 44 University Road
Belfast BT7 1NJ, UK
Phone: +44 28 9020 2290

#46
Flour Power
Cuisines: Sandwiches
Average price: £11-25
Address: 39 Donegall Pass
Belfast BT7 1DQ, UK
Phone: +44 28 9031 3555

#47
Scalini Restaurant
Cuisines: Italian, Pizza
Average price: £11-25
Address: 85 Botanic Avenue
Belfast BT7 1JL, UK
Phone: +44 28 9032 0303

#48
Monte Carlo
Cuisines: Fast Food, Fish & Chips
Average price: £11-25
Address: 147 Lisburn Road
Belfast BT9 7AG, UK
Phone: +44 28 9068 7888

#49
Chubby Cherub
Cuisines: Pizza, Italian
Average price: £11-25
Address: Upper Arthur Street
Belfast BT1 4GH, UK
Phone: +44 28 9024 9009

#50
Darcy's Restaurant
Cuisines: British, European
Average price: £26-45
Address: 10 Bradbury Place
Belfast BT7 1RS, UK
Phone: +44 28 9032 4040

#51
Dragon Rendevous
Cuisines: Chinese
Average price: £26-45
Address: 71-75 Donegall Passage
Belfast BT7 1DR, UK
Phone: +44 28 9032 8668

#52
Thai Village
Cuisines: Thai
Average price: £11-25
Address: 50 Dublin Road
Belfast BT2 7HN, UK
Phone: +44 28 9024 9269

#53
Cafe Conor
Cuisines: Breakfast & Brunch
Average price: £11-25
Address: 11a Stranmillis Road
Belfast BT9 5AF, UK
Phone: +44 28 9066 3266

#54
Hakka Noodles
Cuisines: Chinese, Asian Fusion
Average price: Under £10
Address: 15 Clarence Street
Belfast BT2 8DY, UK
Phone: +44 28 9031 3270

#55
Speranza Pizzeria
Cuisines: Italian, Pizza
Average price: £11-25
Address: 16-17 Shaftesbury Square
Belfast BT2 7DB, UK
Phone: +44 28 9023 0213

#56
The Cloth Ear
Cuisines: Pub, British
Average price: £11-25
Address: 35 Waring Street
Belfast BT1 2DY, UK
Phone: +44 28 9026 2719

#57
Little Italy
Cuisines: Fast Food
Average price: Under £10
Address: 13 Amelia Street
Belfast BT2 7GS, UK
Phone: +44 28 9031 4914

#58
AM:PM
Cuisines: Champagne Bar, European
Average price: £11-25
Address: 67-69 Botanic Avenue
Belfast BT7 1, UK
Phone: +44 28 9023 9443

#59
King's Chippy
Cuisines: Fish & Chips
Average price: Under £10
Address: 351 Ormeau Road
Belfast BT7 3GL, UK
Phone: +44 28 9064 6677

#60
McHugh's
Cuisines: Irish, Pub
Average price: £11-25
Address: 29-31 Queens Square
Belfast BT1 3FG, UK
Phone: +44 28 9050 9999

#61
Oodles Loves Noodles
Cuisines: Asian Fusion, Fast Food
Average price: Under £10
Address: 46 Botanic Avenue
Belfast BT7 1JR, UK
Phone: +44 28 9033 2129

#62
La Tasca
Cuisines: Spanish
Average price: £11-25
Address: Queens Quay
Belfast BT3 9QQ, UK
Phone: +44 28 9073 8241

#63
The Dark Horse
Cuisines: Coffee & Tea, Sandwiches
Average price: Under £10
Address: 30-34 Hill Street
Belfast BT15 1, UK
Phone: +44 28 9023 7807

#64
Basement Bar & Grill
Cuisines: Pub, British, Burgers
Average price: £11-25
Address: 18 Donegall Sq E
Belfast BT1 5HE, UK
Phone: +44 28 9033 1925

#65
Malmaison
Cuisines: Beer, Wine & Spirits, British
Average price: £26-45
Address: 34-38 Victoria Street
Belfast BT1 3GH, UK
Phone: +44 28 9022 0200

#66
Chalco's Mexican Grill
Cuisines: Mexican
Average price: Under £10
Address: 112 Lisburn Road
Belfast BT9 6AH, UK
Phone: +44 28 9068 7338

#67
Porterhouse
Cuisines: Steakhouses, European
Average price: Above £46
Address: 245 Lisburn Road
Belfast BT9 7EN, UK
Phone: +44 28 9038 2211

#68
The Other Place
Cuisines: Diners, Breakfast & Brunch
Average price: Under £10
Address: 79 Botanic Avenue
Belfast BT7 1JL, UK
Phone: +44 28 9020 7200

#69
Gingeroot
Cuisines: Indian
Average price: £11-25
Address: 75 Great Victoria Street
Belfast BT2 7AF, UK
Phone: +44 28 9031 3124

#70
La Cuisine
Cuisines: Delis, Breakfast & Brunch
Average price: Above £46
Address: 648 Antrim Rd
Belfast BT15 5GP, UK
Phone: +44 28 9077 8263

#71
Bengal Brasserie
Cuisines: Indian
Average price: £26-45
Address: 322 Lisburn Road
Belfast BT9 6GH, UK
Phone: +44 28 9068 1255

#72
China China
Cuisines: Buffets, Chinese
Average price: Under £10
Address: 1 University Street
Belfast BT7 1FY, UK
Phone: +44 28 9032 0100

#73
Belfast Castle
Cuisines: Caterers, European,
Venues & Event Spaces
Average price: £26-45
Address: Antrim Road
Belfast BT15 5GR, UK
Phone: +44 28 9077 6925

#74
AM:PM
Cuisines: Champagne Bar,
Mediterranean, Lounge
Average price: £11-25
Address: 42 Upper Arthur St
Belfast BT1 4GH, UK
Phone: +44 28 9024 9009

#75
Archana Restaurant
Cuisines: Indian, Pakistani
Average price: £11-25
Address: 53 Dublin Road
Belfast BT2 7HE, UK
Phone: +44 28 9032 3713

#76
The Proper Pasty Company
Cuisines: British, Food
Average price: Under £10
Address: 29 - 31 Queens Arcade
Belfast BT1 3FE, UK
Phone: +44 28 9075 4339

#77
The Windmill
Cuisines: Breakfast & Brunch,
Average price: Under £10
Address: 19-21 Church Lane
Belfast BT1 4QN, UK
Phone: +44 28 9032 5560

#78
The Pharaoh
Cuisines: Turkish, Mediterranean
Average price: Under £10
Address: 9 Elesington Court
Belfast BT6 9JY, UK
Phone: +44 28 9040 1670

#79
The Bethany
Cuisines: Fish & Chips
Address: 246 Newtownards Road
Belfast BT4 1HB, UK
Phone: +44 28 9045 4498

#80
The Bar and Grill
Cuisines: Bar, British
Average price: £26-45
Address: 21 James Street South
Belfast BT2 7GA, UK
Phone: +44 28 9560 0700

#81
Cosmo Belfast
Cuisines: Asian Fusion
Average price: £11-25
Address: R2 R5 Victoria Square
Belfast BT1 4QG, UK
Phone: +44 28 9023 6660

#82
Beatties Supper Saloon
Cuisines: Fish & Chips
Address: 220 Shankill Road
Belfast BT13 2BJ, UK
Phone: +44 28 9024 0273

#83
Little Fat Buddha
Cuisines: Asian Fusion, Fast Food
Average price: £11-25
Address: 269 Upper Newtownards Road
Belfast BT4 3JF, UK
Phone: +44 28 9065 0777

#84
Springsteens Diner
Cuisines: American, Diners
Average price: £11-25
Address: 75 Botanic Avenue
Belfast BT7 1JL, UK
Phone: +44 28 9032 2227

#85
Coco
Cuisines: American
Average price: £26-45
Address: 7 Linenhall Street
Belfast BT2 8AA, UK
Phone: +44 28 9031 1150

#86
Queens Cafe Bar
Cuisines: Pub, European, Irish
Average price: £11-25
Address: 4 Queens Arcade
Belfast BT1 5FF, UK
Phone: +44 28 9024 9105

#87
Cafe Vaudeville
Cuisines: Cafe
Average price: £11-25
Address: 4 Arthur Street
Belfast BT1 4GD, UK
Phone: +44 28 9043 9160

#88
Shu
Cuisines: European, British
Average price: Above £46
Address: 253 Lisburn Road
Belfast BT9 7EN, UK
Phone: +44 28 9038 1655

#89
Mad Hatter Coffee Shop
Cuisines: British, Coffee & Tea
Average price: Under £10
Address: 2 Eglantine Avenue
Belfast BT9 6DX, UK
Phone: +44 28 9068 3461

#90
Cafe Arirang
Cuisines: Korean, Sandwiches
Average price: £11-25
Address: 32 Botanic Avenue
Belfast BT7 1JQ, UK
Phone: +44 28 9032 4513

#91
Teatro
Cuisines: Mediterranean, Italian
Address: 17 Botanic Avenue
Belfast BT7 1JG, UK
Phone: +44 28 9024 4090

#92
The Burrito Bar
Cuisines: Mexican
Average price: Under £10
Address: 118 Andersonstown Road
Belfast BT11 9BX, UK
Phone: +44 28 9030 1257

#93
Welcome Chinese Restaurant
Cuisines: Dim Sum
Average price: £26-45
Address: 22 Stranmillis Road
Belfast BT9 5AA, UK
Phone: +44 28 9038 1359

#94
Pronto
Cuisines: Coffee & Tea, Delis, Sandwiches
Address: 32-36 Dublin Road
Belfast BT2 7HN, UK
Phone: +44 28 9027 8969

#95
Sinnamon
Cuisines: Coffee & Tea, Sandwiches
Address: 49 Botanic Avenue
Belfast BT7 1JL, UK
Phone: +44 28 9031 4816

#96
Ventnors Gourmet
Cuisines: Sandwiches, Coffee & Tea
Average price: Under £10
Address: Bedford Street
Belfast BT2 7FD, UK
Phone: +44 28 9031 9330

#97
Guccii Chip
Cuisines: Fast Food, Fish & Chips
Average price: Under £10
Address: 133 Lisburn Road
Belfast BT9 7AG, UK
Phone: +44 28 9066 6456

#98
Drennan's Restaurant
Cuisines: British, European, French
Average price: £11-25
Address: 43 University Road
Belfast BT7 1ND, UK
Phone: +44 28 9020 4556

#99
The Chippie
Cuisines: Fish & Chips
Average price: Under £10
Address: 29 North Street
Belfast BT1 1NA, UK
Phone: +44 28 9043 9619

#100
The Olive Tree
Cuisines: Delis, Cheese Shops, Italian
Average price: £11-25
Address: 353 Ormeau Road
Belfast BT7 3GL, UK
Phone: +44 28 9064 8898

#101
Welcome Chinese Restaurant
Cuisines: Chinese
Address: 657 Antrim Road
Belfast BT15 5, UK
Phone: +44 28 9077 3317

#102
Bithika
Cuisines: Fast Food, Indian
Average price: Above £46
Address: 133 Lisburn Road
Belfast BT9 7AG, UK
Phone: +44 28 9038 1009

#103
The Weo Ping
Cuisines: Chinese
Average price: £11-25
Address: 177 Antrim Road
Belfast BT15 2GW, UK
Phone: +44 28 9074 8745

#104
Soul Food Co
Cuisines: Delis, Delicatessen,
European, Soul Food
Average price: Under £10
Address: 395 Ormeau Road
Belfast BT7 3GP, UK
Phone: +44 28 9064 6464

#105
Essence
Cuisines: Chinese
Average price: Under £10
Address: Lisburn Road
Belfast BT9 7GT, UK
Phone: +44 28 9066 6610

#106
Aldo's Hot Food Carryout
Cuisines: Fast Food
Average price: Under £10
Address: 396 Falls Road
Belfast BT12 6DJ, UK
Phone: +44 28 9024 3500

#107
Rajput
Cuisines: Indian
Average price: Under £10
Address: 461 Lisburn Road
Belfast BT9 7EY, UK
Phone: +44 28 9066 2168

#108
Mannys Carryout
Cuisines: Fast Food
Average price: Under £10
Address: 241 Antrim Rd
Belfast BT15 2GZ, UK
Phone: +44 28 9035 1504

#109
Jellybean Cafe
Cuisines: Coffee & Tea, Sandwiches
Average price: Under £10
Address: 250 Upper Newtownards Road
Belfast BT4 3EU, UK
Phone: +44 28 9047 3725

#110
Printers Cafe
Cuisines: European
Average price: £11-25
Address: 33 Lower Donegall Street
Belfast BT1 2FG, UK
Phone: +44 28 9031 3406

#111
Dukes at Queens
Cuisines: Pizza, European
Average price: £11-25
Address: 65-67 University Street
Belfast BT7 1FY, UK
Phone: +44 28 9023 6666

#112
Horatio Todds
Cuisines: GastroPub
Average price: £11-25
Address: 406 Upper Newtownards Road
Belfast BT4 3EZ, UK
Phone: +44 28 9065 3090

#113
Campbells Cafe/The Pound Cafe
Cuisines: Breakfast & Brunch
Average price: Under £10
Address: 11 Arthur St
Belfast BT1 4GA, UK
Phone: +44 28 9032 2658

#114
Thai Tanic
Cuisines: Thai, Chinese
Average price: Under £10
Address: 2 Eglantine Avenue
Belfast BT9 6DW, UK
Phone: +44 28 9066 8811

#115
Graffitti
Cuisines: Coffee & Tea
Average price: £11-25
Address: 258 Ormeau Road
Belfast BT7 2FZ, UK
Phone: +44 28 9069 3300

#116
El Toro Grill
Cuisines: Steakhouses, Burgers
Address: 12 East Bridge Street
Belfast BT1 3NQ, UK
Phone: +44 7788 807800

#117
Bubbacue
Cuisines: American, Barbeque
Average price: £11-25
Address: 12 Callendar Street
Belfast BT7 1JR, UK
Phone: +44 28 9027 8220

#118
Knead
Cuisines: Pizza, Italian
Average price: Under £10
Address: 53 Upper Arthur Street
Belfast BT1 4GJ, UK
Phone: +44 28 9024 1677

#119
The Potted Hen
Cuisines: Restaurant
Address: 11 Edward St
Belfast BT1 2LR, UK
Phone: +44 28 9023 4554

#120
Bennetts
Cuisines: European, Coffee & Tea
Average price: £11-25
Address: 4 Belmont Road
Belfast BT4 2AN, UK
Phone: +44 28 9065 6590

#121
The Streat
Cuisines: Sandwiches
Address: Wellington Pl
Belfast BT1 6GB, UK
Phone: +44 28 9024 0004

#122
Curry Club
Cuisines: Indian
Average price: £11-25
Address: 42-46 Malone Road
Belfast BT9 5BQ, UK
Phone: +44 28 9066 6955

#123
Hungry Hound 2
Cuisines: Fish & Chips
Average price: Under £10
Address: 405 Ormeau Road
Belfast BT7 3GP, UK
Phone: +44 28 9058 2285

#124
Deanes
Cuisines: Italian
Average price: Above £46
Address: 36-40 Howard Street
Belfast BT1 6PF, UK
Phone: +44 28 9056 0000

#125
Tao Noodle Bar Cafe
Cuisines: Coffee & Tea, Chinese
Average price: Under £10
Address: 79 Dublin Road
Belfast BT2 7HF, UK
Phone: +44 28 9032 7788

#126
The Cultúrlann Café
Cuisines: Breakfast & Brunch,
Fish & Chips
Average price: Under £10
Address: 216 Falls Road
Belfast BT12 6AH, UK
Phone: +44 28 9024 9280

#127
Benedicts Restaurant
Cuisines: American
Average price: Under £10
Address: 7-21 Bradbury Pl
Belfast BT7 1RQ, UK
Phone: +44 28 9059 1998

#128
Red Panda
Cuisines: Chinese
Average price: £11-25
Address: 2 Queens Quay
Belfast BT3 9QQ, UK
Phone: +44 28 9046 6644

#129
Morelli's Pizeria Napoletana
Cuisines: Pizza
Address: 340 Lisburn Road
Belfast BT9 7, UK
Phone: +44 28 9066 5551

#130
Little Wing
Cuisines: Pizza
Average price: Under £10
Address: 322 Lisburn Road
Belfast BT9 6GH, UK
Phone: +44 28 9066 6000

#131
The Moyola
Cuisines: Fish & Chips
Average price: Under £10
Address: 1-5 Limestone Road
Belfast BT15 3AA, UK
Phone: +44 28 9035 1565

#132
Slice
Cuisines: Fast Food, Pizza
Average price: Under £10
Address: 228-230 Upper Newtownards
Road Belfast BT4 3ET, UK
Phone: +44 28 9065 2222

#133
Jennifer's Diner
Cuisines: Diners
Average price: Under £10
Address: 52 Berry Street
Belfast BT1 1FJ, UK
Phone: +44 28 9031 1014

#134
Deanes at Queens
Cuisines: British
Average price: £26-45
Address: 1 College Gardens
Belfast BT9 6BQ, UK
Phone: +44 28 9038 2111

#135
Spud's
Cuisines: Fast Food
Average price: Under £10
Address: 37 Bradbury Place
Belfast BT7 1RR, UK
Phone: +44 28 9033 1541

#136
Café Renoir
Cuisines: Coffee & Tea, British, Pizza
Average price: £11-25
Address: 93-95 Botanic Ave
Belfast BT7 1JN, UK
Phone: +44 28 9031 1300

#137
Mynt
Cuisines: Dance Club, GastroPub
Average price: Under £10
Address: 2 -16 Dunbar St
Belfast BT1 2LH, UK
Phone: +44 28 9023 4520

#138
Soda Joes
Cuisines: American
Average price: £11-25
Address: Queens Quay
Belfast BT3 9DT, UK
Phone: +44 28 9045 8555

#139
Joy Inn
Cuisines: Chinese
Average price: Under £10
Address: 25-33 Dublin Rd
Belfast BT2 7HB, UK
Phone: +44 28 9023 2485

#140
The Square
Cuisines: French
Average price: £26-45
Address: 89 Dublin Road
Belfast BT2 7HF, UK
Phone: +44 28 9023 9933

#141
Metro Brasserie
Cuisines: European
Average price: £11-25
Address: 13 Lower Crescent
Belfast BT7 1NR, UK
Phone: +44 28 9032 0646

#142
Avoca
Cuisines: European, Delis
Average price: £26-45
Address: 41 Arthur Street
Belfast BT1 4GB, UK
Phone: +44 28 9027 9950

#143
Captain Cod's
Cuisines: Fish & Chips
Average price: Under £10
Address: 13 Summerhill Avenue
Belfast BT5 7HD, UK
Phone: +44 28 9048 0888

#144
Pak Lok Chinese
Cuisines: Chinese
Address: 145 Lisburn Road
Belfast BT9 7AG, UK
Phone: +44 28 9068 3889

#145
Lansdowne Court Hotel
Cuisines: Hotel, European,
Venues & Event Spaces
Average price: £11-25
Address: 657 Antrim Road
Belfast BT15 4EF, UK
Phone: +44 28 9077 3317

#146
Yummy Sandwiches
Cuisines: Sandwiches
Address: Upper Queen Street
Belfast BT1 6DW, UK
Phone: +44 28 9031 2881

#147
Tony Romas
Cuisines: American
Address: 27 University Road
Belfast BT7 1NA, UK
Phone: +44 28 9032 6777

#148
21 Social
Cuisines: Bar, Irish, GastroPub
Average price: Under £10
Address: 1 Hill Street
Belfast BT15 1, UK
Phone: +44 28 9024 1415

#149
Queen's Cafe Bar
Cuisines: European, Fish & Chips
Address: Queens Arcade
Belfast BT1 1, UK
Phone: +44 28 9024 9105

#150
Subway
Cuisines: Sandwiches
Address: 52 Dublin Rd
Belfast BT2 7HE, UK
Phone: +44 28 9023 8898

#151
McCrackens
Cuisines: Irish, Pub
Average price: £11-25
Address: 4 Joy's Entry
Belfast BT1 2, UK
Phone: +44 28 9032 6711

#152
Ground Espresso Bar
Cuisines: Restaurant
Average price: Under £10
Address: 44 Fountain St
Belfast BT1 5EE, UK
Phone: +44 28 9032 8226

#153
Kathmandu Kitchen
Cuisines: Indian, Vegetarian,
Asian Fusion
Average price: £11-25
Address: 11 Botanic Avenue
Belfast BT7 1JG, UK
Phone: +44 28 9024 9264

#154
The Jharna
Cuisines: Indian
Average price: £11-25
Address: 133 Lisburn Road
Belfast BT9 7AG, UK
Phone: +44 28 9038 1299

#155
Isibeal's Restaurant
Cuisines: Coffee & Tea
Address: 27 High Street
Belfast BT1 2AA, UK
Phone: +44 28 9024 0436

#156
Imperial Chinese Restaurant
Cuisines: Chinese
Address: 96 Botanic Avenue
Belfast BT7 1JR, UK
Phone: +44 28 9080 8833

#157
Le Coop - Made In Belfast
Cuisines: Cocktail Bar, American
Address: 38 Hill Street
Belfast BT1 2LB, UK
Phone: +44 28 9545 8120

#158
The Chester
Cuisines: British, Pub, Lounge
Average price: £11-25
Address: 466 Antrim Road
Belfast BT15 5GE, UK
Phone: +44 28 9077 9376

#159
Europa Foods Ni
Cuisines: Delis
Address: 179 Ormeau Road
Belfast BT7 1SQ, UK
Phone: +44 28 9024 8493

#160
Made in Belfast
Cuisines: British
Average price: £11-25
Address: 23 Talbot Street
Belfast BT1 2LD, UK
Phone: +44 28 9024 4107

#161
Yard Bird
Cuisines: British
Address: 3 Hill Street
Belfast BT1 2LG, UK
Phone: +44 28 9024 3712

#162
Failte
Cuisines: European
Address: 145-147 Falls Rd
Belfast BT12 6AF, UK
Phone: +44 28 9024 3846

#163
Harmony Inn
Cuisines: Chinese
Average price: £11-25
Address: 91-93 Saintfield Road
Castlereagh BT8 7HN
Phone: +44 28 9040 3366

#164
Folklore
Cuisines: Irish
Address: 34 King Street
Belfast BT1 6AD, UK
Phone: +44 28 9031 1951

#165
Bithika Tandoori
Cuisines: Indian
Address: 139 Lisburn Road
Belfast BT9 7AG, UK
Phone: +44 28 9038 1009

#166
Dantes
Cuisines: Sandwiches
Address: 153 Stranmillis Road
Belfast BT9 5AJ, UK
Phone: +44 28 9068 3919

#167
Delaney's
Cuisines: British
Average price: Under £10
Address: 19 Lombard St
Belfast BT1 1RB, UK
Phone: +44 28 9023 1572

#168
Culturlann McAdam O Fiaich
Cuisines: Irish
Address: 216 Falls Road
Belfast BT12 6AH, UK
Phone: +44 28 9096 4181

#169
Murphy Browns Restaurant
Cuisines: European
Average price: £11-25
Address: 186 Cavehill Road
Belfast BT15 5EX, UK
Phone: +44 28 9039 1309

#170
The Filling Station
Cuisines: Ice Cream, Sandwiches
Address: 139 Bloomfield Avenue
Belfast BT5 5AB, UK
Phone: +44 7707 050793

#171
Sole Seafood
Cuisines: Seafood
Address: 613 Lisburn Road
Belfast BT9 7GT, UK
Phone: +44 28 9066 2224

#172
James Street South Restaurant
Cuisines: British, French
Average price: £26-45
Address: 21 James Street South
Belfast BT2 7GA, UK
Phone: +44 28 9043 4310

#173
Ben's
Cuisines: Coffee & Tea, Cafe
Address: 70 Connsbrook Avenue
Belfast BT4 1JW, UK
Phone: +44 28 9067 1945

#174
Ace
Cuisines: Breakfast & Brunch, Burgers
Address: 22 Belmont Road
Belfast BT4 2AN, UK
Phone: +44 28 9047 3333

#175
Five Star
Cuisines: Fast Food
Average price: Under £10
Address: 129 Lisburn Rd
Belfast BT9 7AG, UK
Phone: +44 28 9066 6965

#176
Yangtze Noodle Bar
Cuisines: Chinese
Address: Royal Ave
Belfast BT1 1, UK
Phone: +44 28 9023 3233

#177
The Other Place Express
Cuisines: Diners
Average price: Under £10
Address: 10-12 Queen's St
Belfast BT1 3, UK
Phone: +44 28 9031 4407

#178
St Georges Market Bar & Grill
Cuisines: British
Address: 119 May Street
Belfast BT1 4FG, UK
Phone: +44 28 9024 0014

#179
Neills Hill Brasserie
Cuisines: European
Average price: Above £46
Address: 229 Upper Newtownards Road
Belfast BT4 3JH, UK
Phone: +44 28 9065 0079

#180
Sopranos
Cuisines: Italian
Average price: £11-25
Address: 529 Antrim Road
Belfast BT15 3BS, UK
Phone: +44 28 9077 1062

#181
Cafe Avoca
Cuisines: Brasserie
Average price: Under £10
Address: 10 Bedford Street
Belfast BT2 7FB, UK
Phone: +44 28 9032 6601

#182
Planks Sandwich Co.
Cuisines: Sandwiches
Average price: Under £10
Address: 397 Ormeau Rd
Belfast BT7 3GP, UK
Phone: +44 28 9064 4447

#183
Cutter's Wharf
Cuisines: Restaurant, Lounge
Average price: £11-25
Address: Lockview Road
Belfast BT9 5FJ, UK
Phone: +44 28 9066 3388

#184
Subway
Cuisines: Sandwiches
Address: 62-64 Botanic Avenue
Belfast BT7 1JR, UK
Phone: +44 28 9028 1010

#185
Ravenous
Cuisines: Sandwiches, Coffee & Tea
Average price: Under £10
Address: 3 Stranmillis Road
Belfast BT9 5AF, UK
Phone: +44 28 9066 8988

#186
The Indian
Cuisines: Indian
Address: Upper Newtownards Road
Belfast BT4, UK
Phone: +44 28 904 7388

#187
Pizza Paradise
Cuisines: Pizza, Fast Food
Average price: £11-25
Address: 126 Lisburn Rd
Belfast BT9 6AH, UK
Phone: +44 28 9066 5252

#188
Spur Steak & Grill
Cuisines: Steakhouses
Average price: £11-25
Address: Victoria Square
Belfast BT1, UK
Phone: +44 28 9032 0744

#189
The Eastender
Cuisines: Pub, British
Average price: £11-25
Address: 426 Woodstock Road
Belfast BT6 9DR, UK
Phone: +44 28 9073 2443

#190
The Lonely Poet
Cuisines: GastroPub
Average price: £11-25
Address: Kings Square
Belfast BT5 7EA, UK
Phone: +44 28 9040 1248

#191
Cafe Smart
Cuisines: Coffee & Tea, Sandwiches
Average price: £11-25
Address: 56 Belmont Rd
Belfast BT4 2AN, UK
Phone: +44 28 9047 1679

#192
Blinker's Cafe
Cuisines: British, Breakfast & Brunch
Average price: Under £10
Address: 1 Bridge Street
Belfast BT1 1LT, UK
Phone: +44 28 9024 3330

#193
Brown's Traditional Fish & Chip
Cuisines: Fish & Chips
Average price: Under £10
Address: 119 May Street
Belfast BT1 3JL, UK
Phone: +44 28 9024 6765

#194
City Lite
Cuisines: British
Address: 44 Castle Street
Belfast BT1 1HB, UK
Phone: +44 28 9033 0077

#195
Kookys
Cuisines: Coffee & Tea, Sandwiches
Average price: Under £10
Address: 112 Lisburn Road
Belfast BT9 7, UK
Phone: +44 28 9068 7338

#196
Nando's
Cuisines: Portuguese
Average price: £11-25
Address: Victoria Square
Belfast BT1 4QG, UK
Phone: +44 28 9032 3452

#197
Costa Coffee
Cuisines: Cafe
Average price: £11-25
Address: George Best City Airport
Belfast BT3 9JH, UK
Phone: +44 28 9045 9426

#198
Good Luck Chinese
Cuisines: Chinese, Fast Food, Food
Delivery Services, Cantonese
Average price: Under £10
Address: 173 Kingsway
Belfast BT17 9RY, UK
Phone: +44 28 9062 4662

#199
Cargoes Cafe
Cuisines: Delis, Cafe, Sandwiches
Address: 613 Lisburn Road
Belfast BT9 7GT, UK
Phone: +44 28 9066 5451

#200
Sarnies
Cuisines: Fast Food
Address: 35 Rosemary Street
Belfast BT1 1QB, UK
Phone: +44 28 9024 8531

#201
Jimmy Browns
Cuisines: British, Delis
Address: 1 James St
Belfast BT2 7, UK
Phone: +44 28 9031 9285

#202
Little Wing
Cuisines: Pizza
Average price: £11-25
Address: 10 Ann Street
Belfast BT1 4, UK
Phone: +44 28 9024 7000

#203
Strikes Restaurant
Cuisines: American
Average price: Under £10
Address: 19 Bridge St
Belfast BT1 1LT, UK
Phone: +44 28 9032 0945

#204
The Garden Cafe
Cuisines: British, Coffee & Tea
Average price: Under £10
Address: Botanic Ave
Belfast BT7 1JQ, UK
Phone: +44 28 9033 3188

#205
Chop Sticks
Cuisines: Fast Food, Chinese
Address: 102 Stranmillis Rd
Belfast BT9 5AE, UK
Phone: +44 28 9066 7798

#206
Spud U Like
Cuisines: Fast Food
Address: Castle Ct
Belfast BT1 1DD, UK
Phone: +44 28 9027 1052

#207
Cafe Fish
Cuisines: Fish & Chips
Average price: Under £10
Address: 539 Lisburn Road
Belfast BT9 7GQ, UK
Phone: +44 28 9066 4731

#208
2 Taps Winebar
Cuisines: Spanish, Basque
Average price: £11-25
Address: 30-42 Waring Street
Belfast BT1 2ED, UK
Phone: +44 28 9031 1414

#209
The Belmont Bethany
Cuisines: Fast Food, Fish & Chips
Average price: Under £10
Address: 79 Belmont Rd
Belfast BT4 2AA, UK
Phone: +44 28 9065 7823

#210
Temple Restaurant
Cuisines: British, European
Average price: £11-25
Address: 62 Andersonstown Rd
Belfast BT11 9AN, UK
Phone: +44 28 9020 2060

#211
Linen Hall Library
Cuisines: Library, Cafe
Address: 17 Donegall Square North
Belfast BT1 5GB, UK
Phone: +44 28 9032 1707

#212
S D Bells
Cuisines: Breakfast & Brunch
Average price: Under £10
Address: 516 Upper Newtownards Rd
Belfast BT4 3HL, UK
Phone: +44 28 9047 1774

#213
Hakka Noodle
Cuisines: Japanese
Address: 51 Adelaide Street
Belfast BT2 8FE, UK
Phone: +44 28 9031 3270

#214
Meat in a Bap
Cuisines: Irish, Burgers, Sandwiches
Address: 10 Bedford Street
Belfast BT2 7FB, UK
Phone: +61 2 8903 14905

#215
Deane's Bistro
Cuisines: European
Address: 34 Howard St
Belfast BT1 6, UK
Phone: +44 28 9038 2111

#216
Subway
Cuisines: Coffee & Tea, Fast Food
Address: 6-8 Great Victoria Street
Belfast BT2 7BA, UK
Phone: +44 28 9031 0335

#217
Mace Express
Cuisines: Convenience Stores, Delis
Average price: Under £10
Address: Unit 5
Belfast BT7 2JA, UK
Phone: +44 28 9032 2270

#218
Alan's Causeway Cafe
Cuisines: Breakfast & Brunch,
Coffee & Tea, Bagels
Average price: Under £10
Address: 22-32 Donegall Road
Belfast BT12 5JN, UK
Phone: +44 28 9032 8292

#219
O'Brien's Irish Sandwich Bar
Cuisines: Coffee & Tea, Cafe
Address: 7 Fountain Street
Belfast BT1 5EA, UK
Phone: +44 28 9024 8309

#220
Baltimore Jack's
Cuisines: American
Address: 75 Botanic Avenue
Belfast BT7 1LJ, UK
Phone: +44 28 9002 5860

#221
The Duo
Cuisines: Chinese
Address: 1 Lanyon Quay
Belfast BT1 3LG, UK
Phone: +44 28 9023 7717

#222
Malmaison Brasserie
Cuisines: Brasserie
Address: 34-38, Victoria Street,
Belfast BT1 3GH, UK
Phone: +44 28 9022 0200

#223
The Big Breakfast
Cuisines: Breakfast & Brunch
Address: High St
Belfast BT1 2JZ, UK
Phone: +44 28 9032 9729

#224
Ruchi
Cuisines: Fast Food, Indian
Average price: Under £10
Address: 174 Ormeau Road
Belfast BT7 2ED, UK
Phone: +44 28 9043 4400

#225
Hippodrome
Cuisines: European
Address: Great Victoria St
Belfast BT2 7HR, UK
Phone: +44 28 9024 1919

#226
Aparment Bar & Restaurant
Cuisines: American
Average price: £11-25
Address: 2 Donegal Sq W
Belfast BT1 6JA, UK
Phone: +44 28 9050 4777

#227
Mister Michael's
Cuisines: Fish & Chips
Address: 270 Donegall Road
Belfast BT12 6FW, UK
Phone: +44 28 9033 0733

#228
Polskie Deli
Cuisines: Delis, Grocery
Address: 120 Lisburn Road
Belfast BT9 7, UK
Phone: +44 28 9068 1913

#229
Seasons
Cuisines: British
Address: 2 Woodstock Link
Belfast BT6 8DD, UK
Phone: +44 28 9073 0150

#230
The Abacus
Cuisines: Chinese
Average price: £11-25
Address: 115 Eglantine Avenue
Belfast BT9 6EU, UK
Phone: +44 28 9068 3366

#231
Bishops Restaurant
Cuisines: American
Address: 137 Stranmillis Road
Belfast BT9 5AJ, UK
Phone: +44 28 9038 1234

#232
Wrap Works
Cuisines: Restaurant
Address: 199 Lisburn Road
Belfast BT9 7EJ, UK
Phone: +44 28 9022 1141

#233
The Abacus
Cuisines: Fast Food
Address: 102 Stranmillis Road
Belfast BT9 5AE, UK
Phone: +44 28 9066 7798

#234
Chung Ying
Cuisines: Chinese, Fast Food
Address: 11 Melrose St
Belfast BT9 7, UK
Phone: +44 28 9038 1931

#235
Istanbul Kebab
Cuisines: Fast Food
Address: 269 Woodstock Road
Belfast BT6 8PR, UK
Phone: +44 28 9046 6190

#236
Zafron Restaurant
Cuisines: Indian, Pakistani
Address: 241 Lisburn Road
Belfast BT9 7EN, UK
Phone: +44 28 9058 1155

#237
Subway
Cuisines: Sandwiches
Address: 228 Shankill Rd
Belfast BT13 2BJ, UK
Phone: +44 28 9024 6293

#238
Cagney's
Cuisines: Fish & Chips
Average price: £11-25
Address: 341 Woodstock Road
Belfast BT6 8PT, UK
Phone: +44 28 9045 1255

#239
BT Dine
Cuisines: American
Average price: £11-25
Address: 214 Lisburn Rd
Belfast BT9 6GD, UK
Phone: +44 28 9066 0411

#240
KFC
Cuisines: Fast Food
Address: 419 Lisburn Road
Belfast BT9 7EW, UK
Phone: +44 28 9066 3646

#241
Cracow City Restaurant
Cuisines: Polish
Address: 69 Cregagh Rd
Belfast BT6 8PY, UK
Phone: +44 7799 326509

#242
The Avenue
Cuisines: Fish & Chips
Address: Mountcollyer Avenue
Belfast BT15 3DQ, UK
Phone: +44 28 9075 7899

#243
Nex D'or
Cuisines: British, Breakfast & Brunch
Average price: Under £10
Address: 13 Rosemary St
Belfast BT1 1QA, UK
Phone: +44 28 9032 2711

#244
Wagamama
Cuisines: Asian Fusion
Average price: £11-25
Address: Victoria Square
Belfast BT1 4QG, UK
Phone: +44 28 9023 6098

#245
Nando's
Cuisines: Fast Food
Address: 24 Ormeau Ave
Belfast BT2 8HS, UK
Phone: +44 28 9043 4442

#246
K2 Kebabs
Cuisines: Fast Food
Address: 81 Dublin Rd
Belfast BT2 7HF, UK
Phone: +44 28 9024 9282

#247
Centra Donegal Square West
Cuisines: Coffee & Tea, Delis
Average price: £26-45
Address: 5-6 Donegall Square West
Belfast BT1 6JA, UK
Phone: +44 28 9033 9996

#248
McDonald's
Cuisines: Fast Food
Address: 2/4 Donegall Pl
Belfast BT1 5BA, UK
Phone: +44 28 9031 1600

#249
New Century
Cuisines: Fast Food, Chinese
Address: 37 Belmont Rd
Belfast BT4 2AA, UK
Phone: +44 28 9065 5525

#250
Tao Noodle Bar & Restaurant
Cuisines: Chinese
Average price: £11-25
Address: 1 York Street
Belfast BT15 1ED, UK
Phone: +44 28 9023 6808

#251
Rahmi's
Cuisines: Turkish
Average price: Under £10
Address: 49 Dublin Rd
Belfast BT2 7HD, UK
Phone: +44 28 9033 9988

#252
Bangla Fusion
Cuisines: Indian
Average price: Under £10
Address: 117 Great Victoria St
Belfast BT2 7AH, UK
Phone: +44 28 9024 5431

#253
La Creperie
Cuisines: Creperies, Specialty Food
Address: 12 East Bridge Street
Belfast BT7 2, UK
Phone: +44 28 9032 0202

#254
Deli Delights
Cuisines: Bakery, Sandwiches
Address: 12 East Bridge Street
Belfast BT7 2, UK
Phone: +44 28 9032 0202

#255
Sizzle and Roll
Cuisines: Breakfast & Brunch
Address: 12 E Bridge St
Belfast BT7 2, UK
Phone: +44 28 9032 0202

#256
California Rolls
Cuisines: Japanese, Ethnic Food
Address: 12 East Bridge Street
Belfast BT7 2, UK
Phone: +44 28 9032 0202

#257
Starbucks Coffee
Cuisines: Cafe
Address: 2 Castle Lane
Belfast BT1 5DA, UK
Phone: +44 28 9023 6679

#258
The Streat
Cuisines: Cafe
Address: 66-68 Ann St
Belfast BT1 4, UK
Phone: +44 28 9033 0459

#259
Caffe Uno
Cuisines: Italian
Average price: Under £10
Address: 15 Lombard St
Belfast BT1 1RB, UK
Phone: +44 28 9032 3132

#260
Subway
Cuisines: Sandwiches
Address: 69 Royal Avenue
Belfast BT1 1FE, UK
Phone: +44 28 9032 3759

#261
John Dorys
Cuisines: Fast Food
Average price: Under £10
Address: 220 Holywood Road
Belfast BT4 3BA, UK
Phone: +44 28 9047 3535

#262
Subway
Cuisines: Sandwiches
Address: Castle Ct
Belfast BT1 1DD, UK
Phone: +44 28 9024 2333

#263
Tojo's
Cuisines: Coffee & Tea, British
Address: Winetavern Street
Belfast BT1 1JQ, UK
Phone: +44 28 9032 4122

#264
Triangles
Cuisines: Sandwiches
Average price: Under £10
Address: 133 Lisburn Road
Belfast BT9 7AG, UK
Phone: +44 28 9066 3130

#265
Subway
Cuisines: Fast Food
Average price: Under £10
Address: 141 Lisburn Road
Belfast BT9 7AG, UK
Phone: +44 28 9022 4800

#266
China Express
Cuisines: Fast Food
Average price: Under £10
Address: 1 Knock Road
Belfast BT5 6QD, UK
Phone: +44 28 9040 1872

#267
Harry Ramsden's
Cuisines: Fish & Chips
Address: 100-150 York St
Belfast BT15 1WA, UK
Phone: +44 28 9074 9222

#268
Planet Spice
Cuisines: Indian
Average price: Under £10
Address: 303 Upper Newtownards
Belfast BT4 3JH, UK
Phone: +44 28 9065 4777

#269
**Angela's Sandwich Bar
and Bistro**
Cuisines: Sandwiches
Address: 315 Antrim Road
Belfast BT15 5, UK
Phone: +44 28 9074 0316

#270
Indian Knights
Cuisines: Indian
Average price: Under £10
Address: 158 Cavehill Road
Belfast BT15 5EX, UK
Phone: +44 28 9071 7060

#271
Sea Fry
Cuisines: Fish & Chips
Average price: Under £10
Address: 70 Knockbreda Rd
Belfast BT6 0JB, UK
Phone: +44 28 9064 0867

#272
Golden Fry
Cuisines: Fish & Chips
Average price: Under £10
Address: 450 Shore Road
Belfast BT15 4HD, UK
Phone: +44 28 9037 0246

#273
The Lock Keeper's Inn
Cuisines: Breakfast & Brunch
Address: 2a Lock Keepers Ln
Belfast BT8 7XT, UK
Phone: +44 28 9069 3953

#274
Hong Kong Night
Cuisines: Fast Food, Chinese
Address: 136 Upper Lisburn Road
Belfast BT10 0BE, UK
Phone: +44 28 9061 9031

#275
Snax In The City
Cuisines: Coffee & Tea, Sandwiches
Average price: £11-25
Address: 19 Linenhall St
Belfast BT2 8AA, UK
Phone: +44 28 9031 9631

#276
Upper Crust
Cuisines: Sandwiches
Address: E Bridge St
Belfast BT1 3PB, UK
Phone: +44 28 9024 6962

#277
Pharaoh
Cuisines: Fast Food, Mediterranean
Address: 198 Lisburn Road
Belfast BT9 7, UK
Phone: +44 28 9066 9932

#278
Hong Kong Takeaway
Cuisines: Fast Food
Average price: Under £10
Address: 181 Shankill Road
Belfast BT13 1FP, UK
Phone: +44 28 9032 9422

#279
Cassidy's Restaurant
Cuisines: British
Address: 347-349 Antrim Rd
Belfast BT15 5, UK
Phone: +44 28 9080 5552

#280
Emerald City
Cuisines: Fast Food, Chinese
Address: 59 Dublin Road
Belfast BT2 7HE, UK
Phone: +44 28 9023 5072

#281
Mersin Kebab House
Cuisines: Fast Food
Address: 121 Antrim Rd
Belfast BT15 2BL, UK
Phone: +44 28 9074 7440

#282
Four Star Pizza
Cuisines: Pizza
Address: 205 Lisburn Road
Belfast BT9 7EJ, UK
Phone: +44 28 9066 2999

#283
Night Of Bengal
Cuisines: Fast Food
Address: 313 Antrim Road
Belfast BT15 2HF, UK
Phone: +44 28 9061 6965

#284
Caffe Casa
Cuisines: Coffee & Tea, Cafe
Address: 1 James Street South
Belfast BT2 8DN, UK
Phone: +44 28 9031 9970

#285
Ruby Tuesday's
Cuisines: British
Average price: £11-25
Address: 629 Lisburn Road
Belfast BT9 7GT, UK
Phone: +44 28 9059 3401

#286
Cafe Carberry
Cuisines: Coffee & Tea
Average price: £11-25
Address: 153 Victoria Street
Belfast BT1 4PE, UK
Phone: +44 28 9023 4020

#287
3 Kings Kebab
Cuisines: Turkish, Fast Food
Address: 52 Bradbury Pl
Belfast BT7 1RU, UK
Phone: +44 28 9023 9019

#288
The Fly
Cuisines: Restaurant, Dance Club
Address: 5-6 Lower Cresent
Belfast BT7 1NR, UK
Phone: +44 28 9050 9750

#289
KFC
Cuisines: Fast Food
Address: 33 Ann St
Belfast BT1 4, UK
Phone: +44 28 9024 4076

#290
Bella's Family Restaurant
Cuisines: British
Address: 34 Castle St
Belfast BT1 1HB, UK
Phone: +44 28 9056 2991

#291
Cables Bar
Cuisines: British, Lounge
Address: 4 Lanyon Place
Belfast BT1 3LP, UK
Phone: +44 28 9027 7000

#292
Lagan Palace
Cuisines: Chinese
Address: 136 Ormeau Rd
Belfast BT7 2EB, UK
Phone: +44 28 9023 0135

#293
Oyster Bar
Cuisines: Seafood
Address: Victoria Square
Belfast BT1 4QG, UK
Phone: +44 28 9032 2277

#294
Fryar Tuck
Cuisines: Fish & Chips
Average price: Under £10
Address: 89 Bloomfield Road
Belfast BT5 5LS, UK
Phone: +44 28 9047 1921

#295
Chip 'N Fish
Cuisines: Fast Food
Average price: Under £10
Address: 184 Ravenhill Road
Belfast BT6 8EE, UK
Phone: +44 28 9045 6724

#296
Golden Bell Takeaway
Cuisines: Fast Food
Average price: Under £10
Address: Unit 2
Belfast BT17 0AH, UK
Phone: +44 28 9062 4144

#297
Doorsteps at Conway Mill
Cuisines: Irish, Sandwiches, European
Average price: Under £10
Address: 5-7 Conway Street
Belfast BT13 2DE, UK
Phone: +44 28 9023 7171

#298
Pizza Hut UK
Cuisines: Fast Food, Pizza
Average price: Under £10
Address: Castle Court
Belfast BT1 1DD, UK
Phone: +44 28 9032 9004

#299
Benny's Cafe & Sandwich Bar
Cuisines: Sandwiches
Address: 10 Short St
Belfast BT1 3AF, UK
Phone: +44 28 9074 3128

#300
Golden Kitchen
Cuisines: Fast Food, Chinese
Average price: Under £10
Address: 188 Falls Rd
Belfast BT12 6AG, UK
Phone: +44 28 9062 2026

#301
Beatties Fish Chip Shop
Cuisines: Fish & Chips
Address: 222 Tates Avenue
Belfast BT12 6NB, UK
Phone: +44 28 9032 7222

#302
Crusts
Cuisines: Fast Food, Sandwiches
Address: 224a Tates Avenue
Belfast BT12 6NB, UK
Phone: +44 28 9043 4655

#303
Lyttle Italy
Cuisines: Pizza, Italian
Address: 123 Antrim Rd
Belfast BT15 2BL, UK
Phone: +44 28 9075 4350

#304
Shed
Cuisines: British
Address: 467 Ormeau Road
Belfast BT7 2, UK
Phone: +44 28 9064 2630

#305
The Bread Filler
Cuisines: Sandwiches
Address: 255 Castlereagh Rd
Belfast BT5 5FL, UK
Phone: +44 28 9050 7474

#306
Bridge Traditional Fish & Chips
Cuisines: Fish & Chips
Address: 337 Beersbridge Road
Belfast BT5 5DS, UK
Phone: +44 28 9045 6283

#307
Gallopers
Cuisines: Coffee & Tea, Sandwiches
Average price: Under £10
Address: 46 York Road
Belfast BT15 3HE, UK
Phone: +44 28 9035 6668

#308
Ritchie's
Cuisines: Fast Food
Address: 142 Castlereagh Rd
Belfast BT5 5FS, UK
Phone: +44 28 9046 1525

#309
Peppino Pizzaria
Cuisines: Pizza
Address: 343-345 Antrim Rd
Belfast BT15 2HF, UK
Phone: +44 28 9074 3726

#310
Shanghai Garden
Cuisines: Fast Food
Address: 347 Antrim Road
Belfast BT15 5, UK
Phone: +44 28 9075 6780

#311
Happy House
Cuisines: Fast Food
Address: 355 Antrim Road
Belfast BT15 3BG, UK
Phone: +44 28 9074 6732

#312
Cargoes Delicatessens
Cuisines: Delis
Average price: £11-25
Address: 4 Cranmore House
Belfast BT9 7GT, UK
Phone: +44 28 9066 5451

#313
Manning Inn
Cuisines: Fast Food
Average price: Under £10
Address: 142 Lisburn Road
Belfast BT9 6AJ, UK
Phone: +44 28 9066 3660

#314
Cafe Libra
Cuisines: Coffee & Tea, Sandwiches
Address: 36 Belmont Road
Belfast BT4 2AA, UK
Phone: +44 28 9065 8600

#315
Paella
Cuisines: Spanish
Address: 12 E Bridge St
Belfast BT7 2, UK
Phone: +44 28 9032 0202

#316
Goodfellas Restaurant Pizzeria
Cuisines: Italian
Average price: £11-25
Address: 11 Kennedy Way
Belfast BT11 9AP, UK
Phone: +44 28 9043 1143

#317
Zyton
Cuisines: Fast Food, Indian
Average price: Under £10
Address: 76 Andersonstown Rd
Belfast BT11 9AN, UK
Phone: +44 28 9062 0033

#318
Chopsticks Takeaway
Cuisines: Fast Food
Address: 299 Holywood Road
Belfast BT4 2EX, UK
Phone: +44 28 9067 1223

#319
Supergood
Cuisines: Chinese
Address: 162 Cavehill Road
Belfast BT15 5EX, UK
Phone: +44 28 9071 1643

#320
Doorsteps
Cuisines: Coffee & Tea, Sandwiches
Average price: Under £10
Address: 64 Ann Street
Belfast BT1 4EG, UK
Phone: +44 28 9068 1645

#321
Mandarin City
Cuisines: Chinese
Average price: £11-25
Address: 273-275 Upper Newtownards
Road Belfast BT4 3JF, UK
Phone: +44 28 9080 2888

#322
Subway
Cuisines: Fast Food, Sandwiches
Address: 62 Botanic Ave
Belfast BT7 1JR, UK
Phone: +44 28 9028 1010

#323
KFC
Cuisines: Fast Food
Address: Castle Ct
Belfast BT1 1DD, UK
Phone: +44 28 9024 4076

#324
Gilgamesh Grill
Cuisines: Turkish, Fast Food
Address: 36 Malone Rd
Belfast BT9 6, UK
Phone: +44 28 9066 6345

#325
Red Peach
Cuisines: Fast Food
Address: 50 Upper Newtownards Road
Belfast BT4 3EL, UK
Phone: +44 28 9047 1382

#326
Sunflower
Cuisines: Fast Food
Address: 590 Shore Rd
Belfast BT15 4HG, UK
Phone: +44 28 9078 1578

#327
Ruby Star
Cuisines: Fast Food, Chinese
Average price: Under £10
Address: 229 Castlereagh Rd
Belfast BT5 5FH, UK
Phone: +44 28 9046 1226

#328
The Pizza Place
Cuisines: Pizza
Address: Lenadoon Shops
Belfast BT11 9HF, UK
Phone: +44 28 9060 2909

#329
John Dorys
Cuisines: Fish & Chips
Address: 1 Ballygowan Road
Belfast BT5 7LH, UK
Phone: +44 28 9040 1674

#330
Berries Café
Cuisines: Coffee & Tea, Cafe
Address: 206 Falls Road
Belfast BT11 9, UK
Phone: +44 28 9031 1374

#331
Crystal House
Cuisines: Fast Food, Chinese
Address: 251 Castlereagh Road
Belfast BT5 5FL, UK
Phone: +44 28 9045 9179

#332
Sahara
Cuisines: Fast Food
Address: 35 Botanic Avenue
Belfast BT7 1JG, UK
Phone: +44 28 9059 1222

#333
Avoca Express
Cuisines: Coffee & Tea, Sandwiches
Address: 17 Royal Ave
Belfast BT1 1FB, UK
Phone: +44 28 9024 7774

#334
Salt Bistro
Cuisines: Bistro
Address: Saint Anne's Square
Belfast BT1 2LR, UK
Phone: +44 28 9023 8012

#335
Hill Street Brasserie
Cuisines: Brasserie
Average price: £11-25
Address: 38 Hill Street
Belfast BT1 2LB, UK
Phone: +44 28 9058 6868

#336
Hong Kong Cottage
Cuisines: Fast Food
Average price: Under £10
Address: 37a Stewartstown Road
Belfast BT11 9FZ, UK
Phone: +44 28 9061 4114

#337
Burger King
Cuisines: Fast Food
Address: Castle Court
Belfast BT1 1DD, UK
Phone: +44 28 9032 7790

#338
Rosie's Traditional Fish & Chips
Cuisines: Fish & Chips
Address: Gilnahirk Rd
Belfast BT5 7QL, UK
Phone: +44 28 9070 5505

#339
Brothers Pizza
Cuisines: Pizza, Fast Food
Address: 21 Clifton St
Belfast BT13 1AD, UK
Phone: +44 28 9023 1232

#340
Panda House
Cuisines: Fast Food, Chinese
Address: 124 Lisburn Rd
Belfast BT9 6AH, UK
Phone: +44 28 9066 6599

#341
Cafe Lo-Cal
Cuisines: Restaurant
Address: 273 Woodstock Rd
Belfast BT6 9, UK
Phone: +44 28 9073 8689

#342
Salvezza Pizzeria
Cuisines: Pizza
Average price: Under £10
Address: 192 Falls Rd
Belfast BT12 6, UK
Phone: +44 28 9043 9911

#343
The Streat
Cuisines: Sandwiches
Address: 5 4-6 Boucher Road
Belfast BT12 6HR, UK
Phone: +44 28 9024 3865

#344
Three Bears
Cuisines: Irish, Sandwiches
Average price: Under £10
Address: 455 Ormeau Road
Belfast BT7 3GQ, UK
Phone: +44 28 9049 1636

#345
Roast
Cuisines: Coffee & Tea, Cafe
Address: 58 Wellington Place
Belfast BT1 6GF, UK
Phone: +44 28 9023 4303

#346
Cafe India
Cuisines: Coffee & Tea, Cafe
Address: 42 Malone Road
Belfast BT9 5BQ, UK
Phone: +44 28 9066 6955

#347
The Bridge House - Wetherspoon
Cuisines: British, Pub
Average price: Under £10
Address: 35-43 Bedford St
Belfast BT2 7EJ, UK
Phone: +44 28 9072 7890

#348
Subway
Cuisines: Sandwiches
Address: Boucher Centre Boucher Rd
Belfast BT12 6HR, UK
Phone: +44 28 9066 8449

#349
Clementine
Cuisines: Asian Fusion
Address: 180 Antrim Rd
Belfast BT15 2AJ, UK
Phone: +44 28 9075 7448

#350
Masala
Cuisines: Indian
Address: 186 Antrim Rd
Belfast BT15 2AJ, UK
Phone: +44 28 9075 1871

#351
The Tea Stand
Cuisines: Breakfast & Brunch, Burgers
Address: 12 E Bridge St
Belfast BT7 2, UK
Phone: +44 28 9032 0202

#352
Serendipity Cafe
Cuisines: Breakfast & Brunch, Cafe
Address: 432 Lisburn Road
Belfast BT9 6GF, UK
Phone: +44 28 9068 7382

#353
Lucky Star
Cuisines: Chinese
Address: 76 Andersonstown Rd
Belfast BT11 9AN, UK
Phone: +44 28 9061 7383

#354
Silver House
Cuisines: Fast Food
Average price: £11-25
Address: 185 West Circular Road
Belfast BT13 3QF, UK
Phone: +44 28 9039 1424

#355
Brights Chips & Things
Cuisines: Fast Food
Address: 423 Antrim Road
Belfast BT15 3BJ, UK
Phone: +44 28 9037 1370

#356
KFC
Cuisines: Fast Food
Average price: Under £10
Address: 1-6 Bradbury Place
Belfast BT7 1RS, UK
Phone: +44 28 9032 5129

#357
Freddie's Kitchen
Cuisines: Chinese, Fast Food
Address: 70a Andersonstown Rd
Belfast BT11 9AN, UK
Phone: +44 28 9061 1211

#358
Build a Burger
Cuisines: Burgers
Address: 75 Botanic Avenue
Belfast BT7 1LJ, UK
Phone: +44 28 9023 4595

#359
Welcome Restaurant
Cuisines: Chinese
Average price: £26-45
Address: 65 University Street
Belfast BT7 1HL, UK
Phone: +44 28 9033 1888

#360
Budda 2005
Cuisines: Thai
Address: Unit 4 Queens Quay
Belfast BT3 9QQ, UK
Phone: +44 28 9046 0066

#361
Boston Chinese Take Away
Cuisines: Chinese, Fast Food
Address: 2a Grand Parade
Belfast BT5 5HH, UK
Phone: +44 28 9079 0139

#362
Monzu
Cuisines: Italian, Bar
Average price: £11-25
Address: 701 Lisburn Road
Belfast BT9 7GU, UK
Phone: +44 28 9066 4442

#363
Pizza Hut
Cuisines: Fast Food
Address: 215-225 Castlereagh Road
Belfast BT5 5FH, UK
Phone: +44 28 9073 9000

#364
Windsor Dairy Home Bakery
Cuisines: Bakery, Sandwiches
Address: 4-6 College Street
Belfast BT1 6BT, UK
Phone: +44 28 9032 7157

#365
Deli-licious
Cuisines: Breakfast & Brunch
Average price: Under £10
Address: 373 Beersbridge Road
Belfast BT5 5DT, UK
Phone: +44 28 9073 8090

#366
Bo Win
Cuisines: Fast Food
Average price: Under £10
Address: 592-592a Shore Road
Belfast BT15 4HG, UK
Phone: +44 28 9077 1731

#367
The National Grande Café
Cuisines: Bistro, Breakfast & Brunch
Address: 62-68 High Street
Belfast BT1 2BE, UK
Phone: +44 28 9031 1130

#368
Manlee
Cuisines: Fast Food
Average price: Under £10
Address: 118 Blacks Rd
Belfast BT10 0NF, UK
Phone: +44 28 9061 0203

#369
Baja Taqueria
Cuisines: Mexican
Average price: Under £10
Address: 228 Upper Newtownards Road
Belfast BT4 3ET, UK
Phone: +44 7403 157007

#370
Flame
Cuisines: Bistro, Bar, Delis
Address: 46 Howard Street
Belfast BT1 6PG, UK
Phone: +44 28 9033 2121

#371
Bourbon at Queens
Cuisines: British
Address: 31 University Road
Belfast BT7 1NA, UK
Phone: +44 28 9023 9950

#372
Ox
Cuisines: European
Address: 1 Oxford Street
Belfast BT1 3LA, UK
Phone: +44 28 9031 4121

#373
Four Winds The Bar Restaurant
Cuisines: Restaurant & Wine Bar
Average price: £11-25
Address: 111 Newton Park
Belfast BT8 6LX, UK
Phone: +44 28 9070 7970

#374
Sugarush Caribbean Cuisine
Cuisines: Caribbean
Address: 12-20 E Bridge St
Belfast BT1 3NQ, UK
Phone: +44 7916 474303

#375
Giacomo's Pizza
Cuisines: Cafe, Italian, Fast Food
Average price: £11-25
Address: 42 Malone Road
Belfast BT9 5BQ, UK
Phone: +44 28 9066 5588

#376
Lee Dart Chinese
Cuisines: Chinese
Address: 251 Woodstock Road
Belfast BT6 8PQ, UK
Phone: +44 28 9073 2053

#377
Mandarin Buffet
Cuisines: Chinese, Fast Food, Buffets
Address: Cityside Shopping Centre
Yorkgate Belfast BT15 1WA, UK
Phone: +44 28 9075 4811

#378
Jade House
Cuisines: Chinese
Average price: £11-25
Address: 131 Upper Lisburn Rd
Belfast BT10 0, UK
Phone: +44 28 9061 3163

#379
Shimla Indian Cuisine
Cuisines: Indian
Average price: £11-25
Address: 396 Woodstock Road
Belfast BT6 9DQ, UK
Phone: +44 28 9045 4800

#380
Indian Ocean
Cuisines: Indian
Average price: £11-25
Address: 2 Queens Quay
Belfast BT3 9QQ, UK
Phone: +44 28 9046 6888

#381
Macau
Cuisines: Chinese
Average price: £26-45
Address: 271 Ormeau Road
Belfast BT7 3GG, UK
Phone: +44 28 9069 1800

#382
Good Fortune
Cuisines: Chinese
Average price: £11-25
Address: 402 Upper Newtownards Road
Belfast BT4 3GE, UK
Phone: +44 28 9065 9611

#383
Robinson & Cleaver
Cuisines: Bistro
Average price: £11-25
Address: Donegal Square N
Belfast BT1 5GB, UK
Phone: +44 28 9031 2538

#384
Maze Restaurant
Cuisines: Asian Fusion, European
Address: 11 Wellington Place
Belfast BT1 6GE, UK
Phone: +44 28 9508 6794

#385
Frankie & Bennys
Cuisines: Italian
Address: Unit RO2 Roof Garden
Belfast BT1 4EB, UK
Phone: +44 28 9072 7820

#386
Cafe Metz
Cuisines: Restaurant, Coffee & Tea
Address: 12 Queen Street
Belfast BT1 6ED, UK
Phone: +44 28 9024 9484

#387
Mikey's Deli
Cuisines: American, Food Delivery
Services, Internet Cafe
Address: 6 Belfast BT1 1LU, UK
Phone: +44 28 9508 6858

#388
Ba Soba Noodle Bar
Cuisines: Chinese
Average price: Under £10
Address: 38 Hill Street
Belfast BT1 2LB, UK
Phone: +44 28 9058 6868

#389
Luciano's Cafe Bar
Cuisines: Coffee & Tea, Sandwiches
Address: 2-6 Great Victoria Street
Belfast BT2 7HR, UK
Phone: +44 28 9024 1919

#390
Amici
Cuisines: Italian
Address: 133 Lisburn Road
Belfast BT9 7AG, UK
Phone: +44 28 9066 7990

#391
Tung Sun
Cuisines: Fast Food
Address: 287 Ormeau Road
Belfast BT7 3GG, UK
Phone: +44 28 9049 1678

#392
Baja Taqueria - Fresh Mexican
Cuisines: Mexican
Address: 12-20 East Bridge Street
Belfast BT4 3ET, UK
Phone: +44 7403 157007

#393
Bombay Dreams
Cuisines: Indian
Address: 241Shankill Road
Belfast BT13, UK
Phone: +44 28 9024 2465

#394
Subway
Cuisines: Sandwiches
Address: 436 Woodstock Rd
Belfast BT6 9DR, UK
Phone: +44 28 9073 1216

#395
Caife Feirste
Cuisines: Cafe
Address: Fallswater St
Belfast BT12 6, UK
Phone: +44 28 9096 4184

#396
Bamboo Garden
Cuisines: Fast Food
Average price: £11-25
Address: 22 Woodvale Road
Belfast BT13 3BS, UK
Phone: +44 28 9023 3895

#397
McDonald's
Cuisines: Fast Food
Address: Connswater Retail Park
Belfast BT5 4AF, UK
Phone: +44 28 9045 7599

#398
Chef King
Cuisines: Fast Food
Address: 345 Antrim Road
Belfast BT15 2HF, UK
Phone: +44 28 9074 8152

#399
McDonald's Restaurant
Cuisines: Fast Food
Address: 375 Newtownards Road
Belfast BT5 5DL, UK
Phone: +44 28 9045 7599

#400
D'Angelo's Restaurant
Cuisines: Italian
Address: 601 Lisburn Road
Belfast BT9 7GS, UK
Phone: +44 28 9066 3500

#401
Cheungs
Cuisines: Fast Food
Address: 160 Glen Road
Belfast BT11 8BN, UK
Phone: +44 28 9060 0303

#402
Stan & Olly's
Cuisines: Diners, Burgers
Address: 18 Dublin Road
Belfast BT2, UK
Phone: +44 28 9023 1213

#403
Roscoff
Cuisines: French
Average price: £26-45
Address: 7-11 Linenhall Street
Belfast BT2 8AA, UK
Phone: +44 28 9031 1150

#404
Bagel:Bagel
Cuisines: Cafe
Address: 73 Dublin Road
Belfast BT2 7HF, UK
Phone: +44 28 9033 0487

#405
Deane's Deli
Cuisines: Delis, Food
Average price: Above £46
Address: 44 Bedford Street
Belfast BT2 7EE, UK
Phone: +44 28 9024 8830

#406
Steamboat
Cuisines: Szechuan
Address: 15 Donegall Pass
Belfast BT7, UK
Phone: +44 28 9023 0862

#407
Supreme Hot Food
Cuisines: Fast Food
Address: 62 Sandy Row
Belfast BT12 5EW, UK
Phone: +44 28 9032 4002

#408
Home
Cuisines: British, Delis
Address: 22 Wellington Place
Belfast BT1 6GE, UK
Phone: +44 28 9023 4946

#409
Burger King
Cuisines: Fast Food
Address: 56 Donegall Place
Belfast BT1 5BB, UK
Phone: +44 28 9024 1187

#410
Kebab House
Cuisines: Fast Food
Address: 13-15 Donegall Road
Belfast BT12 5JJ, UK
Phone: +44 28 9032 8567

#411
Nevada Spur
Cuisines: Steakhouses, Burgers
Address: Victoria Square
Belfast BT1 4QG, UK
Phone: +44 28 9032 0744

#412
Maggianos
Cuisines: Italian
Address: Level 2 Victoria Square
Belfast BT1 4QG, UK
Phone: +44 28 9032 1818

#413
Safa
Cuisines: Indian
Address: 30-32 Bank Street
Belfast BT1 1HL, UK
Phone: +44 28 9023 3519

#414
Ginger Cafe
Cuisines: Cafe
Average price: £26-45
Address: Hope Street
Belfast BT12 5EE, UK
Phone: +44 28 9024 4421

#415
Billabong
Cuisines: Fashion, Restaurant
Average price: Under £10
Address: Victoria Square
Belfast BT1 4QB, UK
Phone: +44 28 9032 4533

#416
Portside Inn
Cuisines: Pub, Breakfast & Brunch
Average price: £11-25
Address: 1 Dargan Road
Belfast BT3 9JU, UK
Phone: +44 28 9077 1422

#417
Fat Buddha
Cuisines: Asian Fusion
Average price: £11-25
Address: 92 Lisburn Road
Belfast BT9 6, UK
Phone: +44 28 9068 9777

#418
The Codfather
Cuisines: Burgers, Fish & Chips
Average price: Under £10
Address: 215 Falls Road
Belfast BT11 9, UK
Phone: +44 28 9032 9910

#419
Beatties Fish & Chip Shop
Cuisines: Fish & Chips
Average price: Under £10
Address: 140 Cavehill Road
Belfast BT15 5BU, UK
Phone: +44 28 9024 0273

#420
Raffos Fish Chip Shop
Cuisines: Fish & Chips
Average price: Under £10
Address: 786 Springfield Road
Belfast BT12 7JD, UK
Phone: +44 28 9032 9877

#421
Four Seasons
Cuisines: Chinese
Average price: £11-25
Address: 61-63 Dublin Road
Belfast BT2 7HE, UK
Phone: +44 28 9031 1318

#422
Bagel Bagel
Cuisines: Fast Food,
Coffee & Tea, Bagels
Average price: Under £10
Address: 60 Donegall Street
Belfast BT1 2GT, UK
Phone: +44 28 9024 2545

#423
Golden Bowl
Cuisines: Fast Food
Average price: Under £10
Address: 10 Suffolk Road
Belfast BT11 9PD, UK
Phone: +44 28 9062 0007

#424
Urban Soul
Cuisines: British, Coffee & Tea
Average price: Under £10
Address: 23 May St
Belfast BT1 4NU, UK
Phone: +44 28 9032 5554

#425
Springsteen's Easy Diner
Cuisines: American,
Breakfast & Brunch, Burgers
Average price: £11-25
Address: 633 Lisburn Road
Belfast BT9 7GT, UK
Phone: +44 28 9066 7272

#426
Gaze
Cuisines: Chinese, Malaysian
Average price: Under £10
Address: 415 Ormeau Road
Belfast BT7 3GP, UK
Phone: +44 28 9069 4293

#427
Helen's
Cuisines: Bakery, Breakfast & Brunch
Average price: Under £10
Address: 162 Ormeau Road
Belfast BT7 2ED, UK
Phone: +44 28 9024 1680

#428
Bombay Brasserie
Cuisines: Indian
Average price: Under £10
Address: 241 Lisburn Road
Belfast BT9 7EN, UK
Phone: +44 28 9543 8940

#429
Deli-Lites
Cuisines: Delis, Coffee & Tea
Average price: Under £10
Address: 24-24 Lombard Street
Belfast BT1 1RD, UK
Phone: +44 28 9027 8679

#430
Harbour View Restaurant
Cuisines: Japanese
Average price: Above £46
Address: 1 Lanyon Quay
Belfast BT1 3LG, UK
Phone: +44 28 9023 8823

#431
Peppers Sandwich Bar
Cuisines: Fast Food
Average price: £11-25
Address: 91 Boucher Road
Belfast BT12 6HR, UK
Phone: +44 28 9066 2131

#432
Gourmet Burger Kitchen
Cuisines: Burgers
Average price: Under £10
Address: 1 Victoria Sq
Belfast BT1 4QG, UK
Phone: +44 28 9024 6681

#433
Elements Chinese
Cuisines: Fast Food, Chinese
Average price: £11-25
Address: 239 Antrim Road
Belfast BT15 2GZ, UK
Phone: +44 28 9074 4442

#434
Subway
Cuisines: Sandwiches
Average price: Under £10
Address: 121 Falls Rd
Belfast BT12 6AA, UK
Phone: +44 28 9023 3622

#435
Shanghai Xpress
Cuisines: Fast Food
Average price: Under £10
Address: 119 Andersonstown Rd
Belfast BT11 9BT, UK
Phone: +44 28 9060 4022

#436
Caffe Uno
Cuisines: Italian
Average price: £11-25
Address: 15 Lombard St
Belfast BT1 1RB, UK
Phone: +44 28 9032 3132

#437
The Hercules Bar
Cuisines: Pub, GastroPub
Average price: Under £10
Address: 61-63 Castle St
Belfast BT1 1GH, UK
Phone: +44 28 9033 3905

#438
Alley Cat
Cuisines: Pub, Burgers
Average price: £11-25
Address: Church Lane
Belfast BT1 4QN, UK
Phone: +44 28 9023 3282

#439
The Original Istanbul Kebabs
Cuisines: Fast Food
Average price: Under £10
Address: 145 Ormeau road
Belfast BT7 1SL, UK
Phone: +44 28 9033 2452

#440
Cecil's Sandwich Bar
Cuisines: Sandwiches
Average price: Under £10
Address: 6 Bridge St
Belfast BT1 1LU, UK
Phone: +44 28 9023 6020

#441
Greens Pizza
Cuisines: Pizza, Italian
Average price: £11-25
Address: 549 Lisburn Road
Belfast BT9 7GQ, UK
Phone: +44 28 9066 6033

#442
Arnold's
Cuisines: Fast Food, American
Average price: Under £10
Address: 388 Upper Newtownards Road
Belfast BT4 3EY, UK
Phone: +44 28 9067 1113

#443
Poster Plan
Cuisines: Restaurant
Average price: £26-45
Address: 60 Great Victoria Street
Belfast BT2 7BB, UK
Phone: +44 28 9043 4838

#444
Spires Restaurant
Cuisines: Breakfast & Brunch,
British, Sandwiches
Average price: Under £10
Address: Fisherwick Place
Belfast BT1 6DU, UK
Phone: +44 28 9031 2881

#445
Brights Fish & Chips
Cuisines: Fish & Chips
Average price: Under £10
Address: 23-25 High St
Belfast BT1 2AA, UK
Phone: +44 28 9024 5688

#446
Fontana Restaurant
Cuisines: European, Mediterranean
Average price: £11-25
Address: 61a High Street
Holywood BT18 9AE, UK
Phone: +44 28 9080 9908

#447
The Dirty Duck
Cuisines: Pub, Restaurant
Average price: £11-25
Address: 3 Kinnegar Road
Holywood BT18 9JN, UK
Phone: +44 28 9059 6666

#448
Oxford Exchange
Cuisines: American
Average price: £26-45
Address: St Georges Market
Belfast BT1 4DA, UK
Phone: +44 28 9024 0014

#449
Malone House
Cuisines: European
Average price: £11-25
Address: Malone Road
Belfast BT9 5PB, UK
Phone: +44 28 9068 1246

#450
King Kebab
Cuisines: Fast Food
Average price: Under £10
Address: 195 Falls Road
Belfast BT12 6FB, UK
Phone: +44 28 9033 3336

#451
TGI Fridays
Cuisines: American
Average price: £11-25
Address: Victoria Square Shopping Ctr
Belfast BT1 4QB, UK
Phone: +44 28 9024 9050

#452
Little Wing Pizzeria
Cuisines: Pizza
Average price: £11-25
Address: 201 Upper Newtownards Road
Belfast BT4 3JD, UK
Phone: +44 28 9065 1555

#453
LiLi Wong Chinese Restaurant
Cuisines: Chinese
Average price: £11-25
Address: 159 - 161 Donegall Pass
Belfast BT7 1DT, UK
Phone: +44 28 9024 0575

#454
Camphill Holywood
Cuisines: American
Average price: Under £10
Address: 8 Shore Road
Holywood BT18 9HX, UK
Phone: +44 28 9042 3203

#455
Sunshine Hot Food Bar
Cuisines: Fast Food
Average price: Under £10
Address: 282 Ormeau Road
Belfast BT7 2GB, UK
Phone: +44 28 9069 1926

#456
La Tasca
Cuisines: Spanish
Average price: £26-45
Address: Victoria Square
Belfast BT1 4QG, UK
Phone: +44 845 126 2948

#457
Robert Stewarts Spirit Grocers
Cuisines: European, British
Average price: £26-45
Address: 149 Ballyskeagh Road
Belfast BT17 9BY, UK
Phone: +44 28 9030 8807

#458
The Washington Bar
Cuisines: American
Average price: £11-25
Address: 21 Howard St
Belfast BT1 6NB, UK
Phone: +44 28 9032 3313

#459
Ivory Restaurant & Bar
Cuisines: European
Average price: £11-25
Address: Victoria Square
Belfast BT1 4QG, UK
Phone: +44 28 9032 4577

#460
Chatters Coffee Shop
Cuisines: Coffee & Tea,
Breakfast & Brunch
Average price: Under £10
Address: 64 Bloomfield Avenue
Belfast BT5 5AD, UK
Phone: +44 28 9073 1654

#461
Byblos
Cuisines: Middle Eastern
Average price: £11-25
Address: 8-10 Amelia Street
Belfast BT2 7GS, UK
Phone: +44 28 9023 6266

#462
Enigma
Cuisines: Irish
Average price: £26-45
Address: 2 Sullivan Pl
Holywood BT18 9JF, UK
Phone: +44 28 9042 6111

#463
Moghul Restaurant
Cuisines: Indian
Average price: £11-25
Address: 62a Botanic Avenue
Belfast BT7 1JR, UK
Phone: +44 28 9032 6677

#464
Panini
Cuisines: Delis
Average price: £11-25
Address: 25 Church Road
Holywood BT18 9BU, UK
Phone: +44 28 9042 7774

#465
The Scullery
Cuisines: Fast Food
Average price: £11-25
Address: Unit 7 Kennedy Way
Belfast BT11 9AP, UK
Phone: +44 28 9061 9965

#466
Pavilion Bar
Cuisines: Restaurant,
Pub, Music Venues
Average price: £11-25
Address: 296-298 Ormeau Road
Belfast BT7 2GD, UK
Phone: +44 28 9028 3283

#467
The Whalley Cafe & Gallery
Cuisines: Coffee & Tea, Tapas
Average price: £26-45
Address: 48c High Street
Holywood BT18 9AE, UK
Phone: +44 28 9042 7529

#468
Bengal Brasserie
Cuisines: Indian
Average price: £11-25
Address: 445 Ormeau Road
Belfast BT7 3GQ, UK
Phone: +44 28 9064 7516

#469
The Golden Elephant
Cuisines: Thai
Average price: £26-45
Address: 190 Saintfield Road
Castlereagh BT8 7, UK
Phone: +44 28 9079 6699

#470
Dantes Gourmet Sandwich Bar
Cuisines: Sandwiches
Average price: Under £10
Address: 181 Lisburn Road
Belfast BT9 7EJ, UK
Phone: +44 28 9066 2021

#471
Pizza Express
Cuisines: Pizza, Italian
Average price: £11-25
Address: Victoria Square
Belfast BT1 4QG, UK
Phone: +44 28 9031 4449

#472
Pizza Hut
Cuisines: Pizza
Average price: £11-25
Address: Victoria Sq
Belfast BT1 4QG, UK
Phone: +44 28 9032 1430

#473
Coast
Cuisines: American, British
Average price: £11-25
Address: 30 High Street
Holywood BT18 9AD, UK
Phone: +44 28 9042 3950

#474
Brights Restaurant
Cuisines: Irish
Average price: Under £10
Address: 23-25 High Street
Belfast BT1 2AA, UK
Phone: +44 28 9024 5688

#475
Moghul Indian Carryout
Cuisines: Fast Food, Indian
Average price: Under £10
Address: 66 Andersonstown Road
Belfast BT11 9AN, UK
Phone: +44 28 9060 3613

#476
The House
Cuisines: Pub, European
Average price: £26-45
Address: 12 Stranmillis Road
Belfast BT9 5AA, UK
Phone: +44 28 9068 2266

#477
Kelstar Hot Food Bar
Cuisines: Fast Food
Average price: Under £10
Address: 133A Andersonstown Road
Belfast BT11 9QR, UK
Phone: +44 28 9060 5755

#478
Wine & Co
Cuisines: Wine & Spirits, GastroPub
Average price: £11-25
Address: 57 High Street
Holywood BT18 9AQ, UK
Phone: +44 28 9042 6083

#479
Bright's Restaurant
Cuisines: Irish, Fish & Chips
Average price: Under £10
Address: 41-43 Castle St
Belfast BT1 1GH, UK
Phone: +44 28 9031 0556

#480
Red Panda
Cuisines: Chinese
Average price: £11-25
Address: 60 Great Victoria Street
Belfast BT2 7BB, UK
Phone: +44 28 9080 8700

#481
Barista
Cuisines: Sandwiches
Average price: Under £10
Address: Upper Newtownards Rd
Belfast BT4 3EU, UK
Phone: +44 28 9065 5332

#482
Frankie and Bennys
Cuisines: American, Italian
Average price: £11-25
Address: Victoria Square Shopping Center
Belfast BT1 4, UK
Phone: +44 28 9072 7820

#483
Esperanto
Cuisines: Fast Food, Turkish
Average price: Under £10
Address: 158 Lisburn Rd
Belfast BT9 6AJ, UK
Phone: +44 28 9059 0888

#484
Silk
Cuisines: Chinese
Average price: Above £46
Address: 188 Saintfield Road
Castlereagh BT8 7, UK
Phone: +44 28 9070 1688

#485
Roundabout Hot Food Bar
Cuisines: Fast Food
Average price: Under £10
Address: 156 Glen Rd
Belfast BT11 8BN, UK
Phone: +44 28 9061 1116

#486
Wok Oriental
Cuisines: Chinese
Average price: Under £10
Address: 29 Bradbury Place
Belfast BT2 7BD, UK
Phone: +44 28 9031 3389

#487
Caffe Carlitos
Cuisines: Italian
Average price: £11-25
Address: 78-80 Botanic Avenue
Belfast BT7 1JR, UK
Phone: +44 28 9024 2020

#488
Urban Retreat Sandwich Co
Cuisines: Coffee & Tea, Sandwiches
Average price: Under £10
Address: 7 - 11 Linenhall St
Belfast BT2 8AA, UK
Phone: +44 28 9024 4576

#489
Subway
Cuisines: Sandwiches
Average price: £11-25
Address: 200 Andersonstown Rd
Belfast BT11 9EB, UK
Phone: +44 28 9061 3209

#490
Castle Hill Carryout
Cuisines: Fast Food
Average price: Under £10
Address: 224 Upper Newtownards Road
Belfast BT4 3ET, UK
Phone: +44 28 9047 1597

#491
Capers Pizzas
Cuisines: Fast Food, Pizza
Average price: Under £10
Address: 311-313 Upper Newtownards Rd
Belfast BT4 3JH, UK
Phone: +44 28 9065 5550

#492
Pizza Express
Cuisines: Pizza
Average price: £11-25
Address: 551 Lisburn Road
Belfast BT9 7GQ, UK
Phone: +44 28 9068 7700

#493
Brownes Bar & Grill
Cuisines: American, Bar
Average price: Under £10
Address: 91-93 Boucher Road
Belfast BT12 6HR, UK
Phone: +44 28 9066 0995

#494
Chiquito
Cuisines: Mexican
Average price: £11-25
Address: Victoria Square
Belfast BT1 4QG, UK
Phone: +44 28 9043 6770

#495
Sun Kee
Cuisines: Chinese
Average price: £11-25
Address: 43-47 Donegall Passage
Belfast BT7 1DQ, UK
Phone: +44 28 9031 2016

#496
China Buffet King
Cuisines: Chinese
Average price: Under £10
Address: Victoria Square
Belfast BT1 4GQ, UK
Phone: +44 28 9024 8100

#497
Cafe Naz
Cuisines: Indian
Average price: Under £10
Address: 393 Ormeau Road
Belfast BT7 3GP, UK
Phone: +44 28 9064 8635

#498
All Seasons Restaurant
Cuisines: Chinese
Average price: £11-25
Address: 96 Botanic Ave
Belfast BT2 1JR, UK
Phone: +44 28 9080 8833

#499
China Buffet King
Cuisines: Chinese, Buffets
Average price: £11-25
Address: Victoria Square
Belfast BT1 4QG, UK
Phone: +44 28 9024 8100

#500
Other Place
Cuisines: European
Average price: £11-25
Address: 537 Lisburn Road
Belfast BT9 7GQ, UK
Phone: +44 28 9020 7800

TOP 200 ATTRACTIONS
Recommended by Locals & Trevelers
(From #1 to #200)

#1
Belfast City Hall
Category: Historical Building
Address: Donegall Square
Belfast BT1 5, UK

#2
Botanic Gardens
Category: Botanical Garden, Park
Address: Botanic Avenue
Belfast BT7 1LP, UK
Phone: +44 28 9031 4762

#3
Linen Hall Library
Category: Library, Cafe
Address: 17 Donegall Square North
Belfast BT1 5GB, UK
Phone: +44 28 9032 1707

#4
Belfast Giants
Category: Sports Club
Address: 2 Queen's Quay
Belfast BT3 9QQ, UK
Phone: +44 28 9046 0044

#5
Queen's University
McClay Library
Category: Universities, Library
Address: 10 College Park
Belfast BT7 1LP, UK

#6
W5
Category: Kids Activities
Address: 2 Queen's Quay
Belfast BT3 9QQ, UK
Phone: +44 28 9046 7700

#7
Titanic's Dock and
Pump-House
Category: Historical Building
Address: NI Science Park
Belfast BT3 9DT, UK
Phone: +44 28 9073 7813

#8
Ormeau Park
Category: Tennis, Park, Soccer
Address: Ormeau Road
Belfast BT7 3, UK

#9
Albert Memorial Clock
Category: Landmark
& Historical Building
Address: Queens Square
Belfast BT1 3FF, UK
Phone: +44 28 9024 6609

#10
Cavehill Country Park
Category: Park
Address: Cavehill Road
Belfast BT15 5, UK
Phone: +44 28 9077 6925

#11
The Searcher
Category: Landmark
& Historical Building
Address: 4-12 Holywood Road Belfast
BT4 1NT, UK

#12
Shankill Leisure Centre
Category: Leisure Center
Address: 100 Shankill Road
Belfast BT13 2BD, UK
Phone: +44 28 9091 8750

#13
Stormont Play Park
Category: Playground
Address: Upper Newtownards Road
Belfast BT4 3XX, UK
Phone: +44 28 9072 6345

#14
Invest NI
Category: Public Services
Address: Bedford Square
Belfast BT2 7ES, UK
Phone: +44 28 9069 8000

#15
Stormont Park
Category: Park
Address: Upper Newtownards Road
Belfast BT4, UK
Phone: +44 28 9065 1066

#16
Belfast Central Library
Category: Library
Address: Royal Avenue
Belfast BT1 1EA, UK
Phone: +44 28 9050 9117

#17
Odyssey Bowl
Category: Bowling
Address: 2 Queen's Quay
Belfast BT3 9QQ, UK
Phone: +44 28 9045 2100

#18
Belfast Botanic Gardens
Category: Park
Address: College Park
Belfast BT7, UK
Phone: +44 7767 271683

#19
**The Clock
at the Fountain Centre**
Category: Landmark
& Historical Building
Address: Fountain St
Belfast BT1 6ET, UK

#20
PEC at Queen's
Category: Swimming Pool, Soccer
Address: Botanic Gardens
Belfast BT9 5EX, UK
Phone: +44 28 9068 1126

#21
Ormeau Road Library
Category: Library
Address: Ormeeau Embankment Belfast
BT7 3GG, UK
Phone: +44 28 9050 9228

#22
Neil Pilates
Category: Pilates
Address: University Street
Belfast BT7 1, UK
Phone: +44 7919 172941

#23
Belmont Park
Category: Park, Playground
Address: Cairnburn Road
Belfast BT4 3DU, UK
Phone: +44 7721 537410

#24
Cotswold
Category: Hobby Shop
Address: 7-11 Castle Lane
Belfast BT1 5DB, UK
Phone: +44 28 9024 8607

#25
**Indoor Tennis Centre
& Ozone Complex**
Category: Tennis, Climbing
Address: Ormeau Embankment
Belfast BT6 8LT, UK
Phone: +44 28 9045 8024

#26
Belfast Central Library
Category: Library
Address: Royal Avenua
Belfast BT1 1EA, UK
Phone: +44 28 9050 9199

#27
Ulster Rugby
Category: Sports Club
Address: 85 Ravenhill Park
Belfast BT6 0DG, UK
Phone: +44 28 9049 3222

#28
Waterworks
Category: Park
Address: Antrim Road
Belfast BT14 6, UK
Phone: +44 7887 743923

#29
Central Library
Category: Library
Address: Royal Avenue
Belfast BT1 1EA, UK
Phone: +44 28 9050 9150

#30
Robinson Centre
Category: Leisure Center
Address: Montgomery Road
Belfast BT6 9HS, UK
Phone: +44 28 9070 3948

#31
Musgrave Park
Category: Park
Address: Stockmans Ln
Belfast BT9 7, UK
Phone: +44 28 9038 1851

#32
Lagan Lookout Visitors Centre
Category: Historical Building
Address: 1 Donegall Quay
Belfast BT1 3EA, UK
Phone: +44 28 9031 5444

#33
Avoniel Leisure Center
Category: Leisure Center
Address: Avoneil Road
Belfast BT5 4SF, UK
Phone: +44 28 9045 1564

#34
**Andersonstown
Leisure Centre**
Category: Leisure Center
Address: Andersonstown Road Belfast
BT11 9BY, UK
Phone: +44 28 9062 5211

#35
Ballyhackamore Library
Category: Library
Address: 1 Eastleigh Drive
Belfast BT4 3DX, UK
Phone: +44 28 9050 9204

#36
The Celtic Collection
Category: Sporting Goods, Soccer
Address: 30 Ann St
Belfast BT1 4EG, UK
Phone: +44 28 9023 9111

#37
Spirit of Belfast
Category: Historical Building
Address: Arthur Square
Belfast BT1 4FD, UK

#38
Golf Centre, UK
Category: Golf
Address: 163 York Street
Belfast BT15 1AL, UK
Phone: +44 28 9035 2000

#39
Bank of Ireland Building
Category: Historical Building
Address: 94 Royal Ave
Belfast BT1 1, UK

#40
Casement Park
Category: Amateur Sports Teams
Address: 102 Andersonstown Road
Belfast BT11 9BX, UK
Phone: +44 28 9061 3661

#41
Belfast Central Library
Category: Library
Address: Library Street
Belfast BT1 1EA, UK
Phone: +44 28 9050 9117

#42
Pure Gym
Category: Gym
Address: 3 Edward Street St Annes
Square Belfast BT10, UK
Phone: +44 845 026 8254

#43
Ulster Historical Foundation
Category: Library
Address: 49 Malone Rd
Belfast BT9 6RY, UK
Phone: +44 28 9066 1988

#44
The Twilight Zone
Category: Amusement Park
Address: 25-27 Dublin Road
Belfast BT2 7HB, UK

#45
Botanic Gardens
Category: Botanic Gardens
Address: Botanic Avenue
Belfast BT7 1, UK

#46
Shankill Road Library
Category: Library
Address: 298-300 Shankill Road
Belfast BT13 2BN, UK
Phone: +44 28 9050 9232

#47
Grove Leisure Centre
Category: Leisure Center
Address: York Street Belfast
Belfast BT15 3HF, UK
Phone: +44 28 9072 6363

#48
Holywood Arches Library
Category: Library
Address: 4 Holywood Road
Belfast BT4 1NT, UK
Phone: +44 28 9050 9216

#49
Drumglass Park
Category: Park, Playground
Address: Lisburn Road
Belfast BT9 7, UK
Phone: +44 7721 537436

#50
HMS Caroline
Category: Historical Building
Address: Queen's Rd
Belfast BT3 9DT, UK
Phone: +44 28 9073 7813

#51
Snakes & Ladders
Category: Playground
Address: 169 Clandeboye Road
Belfast BT5 4, UK
Phone: +44 28 9147 7913

#52
The Ulster Brewer
Category: Historical Building
Address: Waterfront Hall
Belfast, UK

#53
Malone Rugby Football Club
Category: Sports Club
Address: Gibson Park Avenue
Belfast BT6 9GN, UK
Phone: +44 28 9045 1312

#54
Sheep Herder
Category: Historical Building
Address: Waterfront Hall
Belfast, UK

#55
Belfast YMCA Fitness Centre
Category: Leisure Center
Address: 58 Knightsbridge Park
Belfast BT9 5EH, UK
Phone: +44 28 9068 4660

#56
Botanic Train Station
Category: Public Services
Address: Botanic Ave
Belfast BT7 1JG, UK

#57
Botanic Garden
Category: Park
Address: Botanic Garden,
Belfast BT9, UK

#58
Polercise
Category: Dance Studio
Address: 185 Donegal Street
Belfast BT12 5, UK
Phone: +44 7727 224095

#59
Tullycarnet Library
Category: Library
Address: Kinross Avenue
Belfast BT5 7GH, UK
Phone: +44 28 9048 5079

#60
Ballysillan Leisure Centre
Category: Leisure Center
Address: Ballysillan Road
Belfast BT14 7QP, UK
Phone: +44 28 9091 8731

#61
Nevada Bob
Category: Golf
Address: 46 Boucher Crescent
Belfast BT12 6QY, UK
Phone: +44 28 9038 2668

#62
Citigolf
Category: Arcades, Golf
Address: Cromac Square
Belfast BT2 8LA, UK
Phone: +44 28 9023 2232

#63
**Cavehill Adventurous
Playground**
Category: Playground
Address: Belfast Castle
Belfast BT15 5, UK
Phone: +44 28 9077 6925

#64
Odyssey Pavilion
Category: Leisure Center
Address: 2 Queens Quay
Belfast BT3 9QQ, UK
Phone: +44 28 9045 8806

#65
Spirit Health & Fitness Club
Category: Gym
Address: 22 Ormeau Avenue
Belfast BT2 8HS, UK
Phone: +44 28 9032 5454

#66
Belfast Bicycle Workshop
Category: Bike Rentals
Address: 1a Lawrence Street
Belfast BT7 1LE, UK
Phone: +44 28 9043 9959

#67
**Belfast Community
Circus School**
Category: Leisure Center
Address: 23-25 Gordon Street
Belfast BT1 2LG, UK
Phone: +44 28 9023 6007

#68
Falls Leisure Centre
Category: Leisure Center
Address: 15-17 Falls Road
Belfast BT12 4PB, UK
Phone: +44 28 9050 0510

#69
Suffolk Library
Category: Library
Address: Stewartstown Road
Belfast BT11 9JP, UK
Phone: +44 28 9050 9234

#70
Arena Health & Fitness Club
Category: Gym
Address: 100-150 York Gate Shopping
Centre Belfast BT15 1WA, UK
Phone: +44 28 9074 1235

#71
Olympia Leisure Centre
Category: Leisure Center
Address: Boucher Road
Belfast BT12 6HR, UK
Phone: +44 28 9023 3369

#72
Woodvale Park
Category: Park
Address: Woodvale Road
Belfast BT13 3BN, UK
Phone: +44 7771 987652

#73
LA Fitness
Category: Gym
Address: 22 Adelaide Street
Belfast BT2 8GD, UK
Phone: +44 843 170 1079

#74
Falls Library
Category: Library
Address: 49 Falls Rd
Belfast BT12 4PD, UK
Phone: +44 28 9050 9212

#75
**Crusaders Football
& Athletic Club**
Category: Sports Club
Address: St Vincent Street
Belfast BT15 3QG, UK
Phone: +44 28 9037 0777

#76
Colin Glen
Category: Library
Address: Stewartstown Road
Belfast BT17 0AW, UK
Phone: +44 28 9043 1266

#77
City Hall Grounds
Category: Park
Address: City Hall Grounds
Belfast BT1 5GH, UK
Phone: +44 28 9032 3289

#78
**Northern Ireland National
Football Team**
Category: Soccer
Address: Donegall Ave
Belfast BT12 6, UK
Phone: +44 28 9024 4198

#79
CI Mini Rugby
Category: Amateur Sports Teams
Address: Circular Road
Belfast BT4 2, UK

#80
Crescent Gardens Park
Category: Park
Address: Crescent Gardens
Belfast BT7 1NS, UK

#81
Gortin Glen Forest Park
Category: Park
Address: Upper Newtownnords Road
Belfast BT4 3SB, UK

#82
Balmoral Bowling Club
Category: Sports Club
Address: Belvoir Drive
Belfast BT8 7DT, UK
Phone: +44 28 9064 0433

#83
Castlereagh Hill Golf Club
Category: Golf
Address: Upper Braniel Road
Belfast BT5 7TX, UK
Phone: +44 28 9044 8477

#84
Orangefield Park
Category: Park
Address: Orangefield Park
Belfast BT5, UK
Phone: +44 28 9049 1813

#85
Robin Gordon Swimming
Category: Swimming School
Address: Campbell College School
Belfast BT5, UK
Phone: +44 7968 471340

#86
Belfast Fencing Club
Category: Fitness & Instruction
Address: Campbell College
Belfast BT5, UK
Phone: +44 7909 738628

#87
Fortwilliam Golf Club
Category: Golf
Address: Downview Avenue
Belfast BT15 4EZ, UK
Phone: +44 28 9037 0770

#88
Fitness First
Category: Gym
Address: Connswater Link
Belfast BT5 4AF, UK
Phone: +44 870 898 0772

#89
**Hydebank Parks
& Playing Fields**
Category: Sports Club
Address: Newtownbreda Road
Belfast BT1 5AA, UK
Phone: +44 28 9064 9647

#90
**Linfield Football
& Athletic Club**
Category: Sports Club
Address: Donegall Avenue
Belfast BT12 6LW, UK
Phone: +44 28 9024 4198

#91
The Rack & Cue
Category: Sports Club
Address: 159 Antrim Rd
Belfast BT15 2GW, UK
Phone: +44 28 9074 9732

#92
Avoniel Leisure Centre
Category: Leisure Center
Address: Avoniel Leisure Centre
Belfast BT5 4SL, UK

#93
Play Time
Category: Playground
Address: 4 Ashdale St
Belfast BT5 5AX, UK
Phone: +44 28 9002 4974

#94
Cliftonville Golf Club
Category: Golf
Address: 44 Westland Road
Belfast BT14 6NH, UK
Phone: +44 28 9022 8585

#95
**Origin Skin Care Centre
& Day Spa**
Category: Gym, Day Spas
Address: Kings Square
Belfast BT5 7EA, UK
Phone: +44 28 9079 8277

#96
Burn Equestrian
Category: Horseback Riding
Address: Saintfield Road
Belfast BT8 8BH, UK
Phone: +44 28 9040 2384

#97
DW Fitness
Category: Fitness & Instruction
Address: 24 Boucher Rd
Belfast BT12 6HR, UK
Phone: +44 844 249 5340

#98
Victoria Park
Category: Park
Address: Park Avenue
Belfast BT4 1JT, UK
Phone: +44 28 9049 1813

#99
Realta Horse Racing
Category: Horseback Riding
Address: 24 Stranmillis Road
Belfast BT9 5AA, UK
Phone: +44 7513 793957

#100
Centaur Health Studios
Category: Gym
Address: 19 Arthur Street
Belfast BT1 4GA, UK
Phone: +44 28 9024 2680

#101
EFP Gyms
Category: Gym
Address: 155 Northumberland Street
Belfast BT13 2HE, UK
Phone: +44 7840 382955

#102
Namaste Yoga Centre & Clinic
Category: Yoga Centre
Address: 265A Ormeau Road
Belfast BT7 3GG, UK
Phone: +44 28 9022 0888

#103
Belvoir Park Golf Club
Category: Golf Club
Address: 73 Church Road
Belfast BT8 7AN, UK
Phone: +44 28 9064 6714

#104
JEM Swimming School
Category: Swimming School
Address: Avoniel Leisure Centre
Belfast BT5 4SF, UK
Phone: +44 7515 286109

#105
Belfast Boat Club
Category: Sports Club
Address: Loughview Road
Belfast BT9 5FJ, UK
Phone: +44 28 9066 5012

#106
Whiterock Leisure Centre
Category: Leisure Centre
Address: Whiterock Road
Belfast BT12 7RJ, UK
Phone: +44 28 9023 3239

#107
Loughside Recreation Centre
Category: Recreation Centre
Address: Shore Road
Belfast BT15 4HP, UK
Phone: +44 28 9078 1524

#108
LA Fitness
Category: Fitness & Instruction
Address: Milltown Road
Belfast BT8 7XP, UK
Phone: +44 843 170 1085

#109
Shandon Park Golf Club
Category: Golf Club
Address: 73 Shandon Park
Belfast BT5 6NY, UK
Phone: +44 28 9080 5030

#110
Energie Fitness For Women
Category: Gym
Address: 142 Upper Lisburn Rd
Belfast BT10 0BG, UK
Phone: +44 28 9061 8839

#111
Biqram Yoga
Category: Yoga Centre
Address: 9 Queen Street
Belfast BT1 6EA, UK
Phone: +44 28 9027 8256

#112
Belfast Giants Ice Hockey Club
Category: Ice Hockey Club
Address: 2 Ormeau Business Park
Belfast BT7 2JA, UK
Phone: +44 28 9059 1111

#113
Ulster Sports Club
Category: Sports Club
Address: High Street
Belfast BT1 2BG, UK
Phone: +44 28 9023 0771

#114
Mayfield Leisure Centre
Category: Leisure Centre
Address: Mays Meadow
Belfast BT1 3PH, UK
Phone: +44 28 9024 1633

#115
Sandy Row Library
Category: Library
Address: 127 Sandy Row
Belfast BT12 5ET, UK
Phone: +44 28 9050 9230

#116
Bar Library Services
Category: Library
Address: 91 Chichester Street
Belfast BT1 3JP, UK
Phone: +44 28 9024 1523

#117
Outside Health & Leisure Spa
Category: Leisure Centre
Address: 1 Donegall Lane
Belfast BT1 2LZ, UK
Phone: +44 28 9032 4448

#118
American Golf
Category: Golf
Address: Albert Bridge Road
Belfast BT5 4GX, UK
Phone: +44 844 499 1946

#119
Windsor Snooker Club
Category: Recreation Club
Address: 2a Edinburgh Street
Belfast BT9 7DS, UK
Phone: +44 28 9066 0906

#120
Ormeau Golf Club
Category: Golf Club
Address: 50 Park Road
Belfast BT7 2FX, UK
Phone: +44 28 9045 8420

#121
Windsor Lawn Tennis Club
Category: Tennis Club
Address: 37 Windsor Avenue
Belfast BT9 6EJ, UK
Phone: +44 28 9066 5188

#122
Templemore Swim & Fitness Centre
Category: Fitness Centre
Address: Templemore Avenue
Belfast BT5 4FW, UK
Phone: +44 28 9045 7540

#123
Dreamworld Family Entertainment Centre
Category: Entertainment Centre
Address: Glenmachan Place
Belfast BT12 6QH, UK
Phone: +44 28 9020 2300

#124
Charter Youth Club
Category: Youth Club
Address: 21 Bentham Drive
Belfast BT12 5NS, UK
Phone: +44 28 9024 0139

#125
Willowfield Bowling Club
Category: Bowling Club
Address: Gibson Park Gardens
Belfast BT6 9GN, UK
Phone: +44 28 9045 8926

#126
Cregagh Sports Club
Category: Sports Club
Address: Gibson Park Avenue
Belfast BT6 9GL, UK
Phone: +44 28 9045 9440

#127
Victoria College Swimming Pool
Category: Swimming Pool
Address: 1 Marlborough Park
Belfast BT9 6XS, UK
Phone: +44 28 9066 6092

#128
Body Vibes Fitness Studio
Category: Fitness & Instruction
Address: 527 Lisburn Rd
Belfast BT9 7GQ, UK
Phone: +44 28 9066 0137

#129
Beechmount Leisure Centre
Category: Leisure Centre
Address: Falls Road
Belfast BT12 6FD, UK
Phone: +44 28 9032 8631

#130
Glentoran Football Club
Category: Football Club
Address: Parkgate Drive
Belfast BT4 1EW, UK
Phone: +44 28 9045 6137

#131
Forthriver Bowling
& Tennis Club
Category: Sports Club
Address: Woodvale Road
Belfast BT13 3BU, UK
Phone: +44 28 9074 1772

#132
Brantwood Football
& Recreation Club
Category: Football & Recreation Club
Address: Jellicoe Avenue
Belfast BT15 3FZ, UK
Phone: +44 28 9077 2370

#133
Albert Foundry Bowling Club
Category: Bowling
Address: West Circular Road
Belfast BT13 3QB, UK
Phone: +44 28 9071 1420

#134
Cliftonville Bowling Club
Category: Bowling
Address: 13-23 Knutsford Drive
Belfast BT14 6LZ, UK
Phone: +44 28 9074 6622

#135
Ballygomartin Social
& Recreation Club
Category: Social & Recreation Club
Address: 171 Ballygomartin Road
Belfast BT13 3NA, UK
Phone: +44 28 9039 1744

#136
Belfast Bowling Club
Category: Bowling
Address: Deramore Park
Belfast BT9 5JT, UK
Phone: +44 28 9066 0755

#137
Pro Kick Gym
Category: Gym
Address: Wilgar Street
Belfast BT4 3BL, UK
Phone: +44 28 9065 1074

#138
Dundela Football Club
Category: Football Club
Address: Wilgar Street
Belfast BT4 3BL, UK
Phone: +44 28 9065 3109

#139
Castleton Bowling Club
Category: Bowling
Address: 60 Skegoneill Avenue
Belfast BT15 3JP, UK
Phone: +44 28 9077 8042

#140
Cherryvale Playing Fields
Category: Playground
Address: Ravenhill Road
Belfast BT6 8EE, UK
Phone: +44 28 9064 2464

#141
Ewart's Bowling Club
Category: Bowling
Address: Somerdale Park
Belfast BT14 7HD, UK
Phone: +44 28 9071 9469

#142
Balmoral Golf Club
Category: Golf Club
Address: 518 Lisburn Road
Belfast BT9 6GX, UK
Phone: +44 28 9038 1514

#143
Salisbury Bowling Club
Category: Bowling
Address: 41/49 Salisbury Ave
Belfast BT15 5DZ, UK
Phone: +44 28 9077 0549

#144
Ballymacarrett Library
Category: Library
Address: 19-35 Templemore Avenue
Belfast BT5 4FP, UK
Phone: +44 28 9050 9207

#145
Falls Bowling & Tennis Club
Category: Bowling & Tennis Club
Address: 63 Andersonstown Road
Belfast BT11 9AH, UK
Phone: +44 28 9043 1006

#146
Woodstock Road Library
Category: Library
Address: 358 Woodstock Road
Belfast BT6 9DQ, UK
Phone: +44 28 9050 9239

#147
Belmont Bowling Club
Category: Bowling Club
Address: 6a Kincora Avenue
Belfast BT4 3DW, UK
Phone: +44 28 9065 3644

#148
Crusaders F.C.
Category: Soccer
Address: Shore Road
Belfast BT15 3PL, UK
Phone: +44 28 9037 0777

#149
Belvoir Activity Centre
Category: Leisure Centre
Address: 100 Belvoir Drive
Belfast BT8 7DT, UK
Phone: +44 28 9064 2174

#150
**Church Of Ireland Young
Men's Society**
Category: Sports Club
Address: 91-93 Circular Road
Belfast BT4 2GD, UK
Phone: +44 28 9076 0120

#151
Arena Health & Fitness
Category: Gym
Address: 35-39 Finaghy Road North
Belfast BT10 0JB, UK
Phone: +44 28 9062 9789

#152
Belfast Indoor Bowls Club
Category: Bowling
Address: 115 Milltown Road
Belfast BT8 7XP, UK
Phone: +44 28 9064 4397

#153
Golfing Union Of Ireland
Category: Golf
Address: Newtownbreda Road
Belfast BT8 6AW, UK
Phone: +44 28 9049 1891

#154
Open Fairways
Category: Golf
Address: Teal Pavillion Portside
Business Park Belfast BT3 9ED
Phone: +44 28 9073 1055

#155
Oldpark Road Library
Category: Library
Address: 46 Oldpark Road
Belfast BT14 6FR, UK
Phone: +44 28 9050 9226

#156
St Galls G A A Club
Category: Sports Club
Address: 4 Milltown Row
Belfast BT12 6EU, UK
Phone: +44 28 9062 5505

#157
Knockbracken Golf Academy
Category: Golf
Address: 24 Ballymaconaghy Road
Belfast BT8 6SB, UK
Phone: +44 28 9070 1648

#158
**Mount Ober Golf
& Country Club**
Category: Golf
Address: Ballymaconaghy Road
Belfast BT8 6SB, UK
Phone: +44 28 9079 2108

#159
Colin Valley Golf Complex
Category: Golf
Address: 115 Blacks Road
Belfast BT10 0NF, UK
Phone: +44 28 9060 1133

#160
Tullycarnet Park
Category: Sports Club
Address: Kingsland Park
Belfast BT5 7FB, UK
Phone: +44 28 9048 4099

#161
Mccorley Club
Category: Sports Club
Address: Glen Road
Belfast BT11 8BU, UK
Phone: +44 28 9061 1515

#162
Toy & Book Library Service Headquarters
Category: Library
Address: 78 Mersey Street
Belfast BT4 1EY, UK
Phone: +44 28 9045 7785

#163
Dunmurry Golf Club
Category: Golf
Address: 91 Dunmurry Lane
Belfast BT17 9JS, UK
Phone: +44 28 9030 1124

#164
Dunmurry Golf Club Pro Shop
Category: Golf
Address: 91 Dunmurry Lane
Belfast BT17 9JS, UK
Phone: +44 28 9062 1314

#165
Malone Golf Club
Category: Golf
Address: Upper Malone Road
Belfast BT17 9LB, UK
Phone: +44 28 9061 4917

#166
Brook Activity Centre
Category: Leisure Centre
Address: 25 Summerhill Road
Belfast BT17 0RL, UK
Phone: +44 28 9030 1848

#167
Kilmakee Activity Centre
Category: Leisure Centre
Address: 52a Rowan Drive
Belfast BT17 9QA, UK
Phone: +44 28 9030 1545

#168
Derriaghy Cricket Club
Category: Sports Club
Address: 40 Queensway
Belfast BT17 9HG, UK
Phone: +44 28 9062 8683

#169
Adrenaline Karting
Category: Go Karts
Address: 1 Cedarhurst Road
Castlereagh BT8 7RH
Phone: +44 28 9064 4654

#170
Esporta Health Clubs
Category: Gym
Address: 106 Belfast Road
Holywood BT18 9QY, UK
Phone: +44 28 9076 5000

#171
Jack's Pack
Category: Dog Park
Address: 13 Milfort Avenue
Belfast BT17 9BJ, UK
Phone: +44 28 9060 3692

#172
Redburn Country Park
Category: Dog Park
Address: Redburn Country Park
Holywood BT18 9BA, UK

#173
Belvoir Forest Park
Category: Park
Address: Old Milltown Rd
Castlereagh BT8 7, UK

#174
Rugby Tots
Category: Fitness & Instruction
Address: 106 Belfast Road
Holywood BT18 9QY, UK
Phone: +44 845 313 3242

#175
Colin Glen Forest Park
Category: Park
Address: 163 Stewartstown Rd
Belfast BT17 0HW, UK
Phone: +44 28 9061 4115

#176
Queen's Hall
Category: Leisure Center
Address: Sullivan Place
Holywood BT18 9JF, UK
Phone: +44 28 9127 1200

#177
Cregagh Library
Category: Library
Address: 409-413 Cregagh Road
Belfast BT6 0LF, UK
Phone: +44 28 9040 1365

#178
Holywood Playground
Category: Playground
Address: High St
Holywood BT18 9, UK

#179
Gymnastics With Carole
Category: Fitness & Instruction
Address: 106 Belfast Rd
Holywood BT18 9, UK
Phone: +44 28 9076 5000

#180
Casino Amusements
Category: Amusement Park
Address: Unit 1 Hibernia Street
Holywood BT18 9JE, UK
Phone: +44 28 9042 7747

#181
Lagan Valley Regional Park
Category: Park
Address: Kingsway Belfast BT17 9AL

#182
Lisburn Road Library
Category: Library
Address: 440 Lisburn Road
Belfast BT9 6GR, UK
Phone: +44 28 9050 9223

#183
Ardoyne Libraries
Category: Library
Address: 446-450 Crumlin Road
Belfast BT14 7GH, UK
Phone: +44 28 9050 9202

#184
Rosie Milton
Category: Trainers, Pilates, Yoga
Address: 1974 Bergen St
Brooklyn 11233, UK
Phone: +44 6462 470319

#185
**Fun French & Spanish
LCF Clubs - Kirsti Larsen**
Category: Kids Activities
Address: Belfast BT17 0QH
Phone: +44 28 9062 2440

#186
Foxhill Farm Livery Stables
Category: Horseback Riding
Address: 6 Beechmount Road
Belfast BT8 8AD, UK
Phone: +44 7717 860409

#187
Skegoneill Library
Category: Library
Address: Skegoneill Avenue
Belfast BT15 3JN, UK
Phone: +44 28 9050 9244

#188
Peter Hill Swimming
Category: Swimming School
Address: Main Street
North Down BT18 9EP, UK
Phone: +44 7708 544044

#189
**Drumbo Park
Greyhound Stadium**
Category: Park, Stadium
Address: 57 Ballyskeagh Road
Lambeg Lisburn BT27 5TE
Phone: +44 28 9061 0070

#190
JEM Swim School
Category: Swimming School
Address: Belfast & Holywood
Holywood BT18, UK
Phone: +44 7515 286109

#191
Laganview Golf Centre
Category: Golf
Address: 24 Ballyskeagh Road
Lisburn BT27 5SY, UK
Phone: +44 28 9061 2332

#192
Claire Ferry Yoga
Category: Yoga
Address: 208 Cregagh Road
Castlereagh BT6 9EU
Phone: +44 28 9022 0426

#193
Fitness First
Category: Gym
Address: Shore Road
Newtownabbey BT36 7BS
Phone: +44 28 9086 9888

#194
Cairnmartin Library
Category: Library
Address: Ballygomartin Road
Belfast BT13 3NL, UK
Phone: +44 28 9050 9241

#195
Laganside Tackle
Category: Fishing
Address: 161 Kingsway Dunmurry
Dunmurry BT17 9RY, UK
Phone: +44 28 9062 5931

#196
Holywood Yacht Club
Category: Yacht Club
Address: Kinnegar Road
Holywood BT18 9JN, UK
Phone: +44 28 9042 3345

#197
Holywood Golf Club
Category: Golf Club
Address: Nuns Walk
Holywood BT18 9LE, UK
Phone: +44 28 9042 3135

#198
Laganview Golf Centre
Category: Golf
Address: 24 Ballyskeagh Road
Lisburn BT27 5SY, UK
Phone: +44 28 9061 2332

#199
Chichester Library
Category: Library
Address: 109 Salisbury Avenue
Belfast BT15 5EB, UK
Phone: +44 28 9050 9210

#200
Braniel Library
Category: Library
Address: Glen Road
Belfast BT5 7JH, UK
Phone: +44 28 9079 7420

TOP 250 NIGHTLIFE

Recommended by Locals & Trevelers
(From #1 to #250)

#1
Lavery's
Category: Pub, Pool Hall, Lounge
Average price: £11-25
Address: 12-16 Bradbury Place
Belfast BT7 1RS, UK
Phone: +44 28 9020 0660

#2
Crown Bar Liquor Saloon
Category: Bar
Average price: £11-25
Address: 46 Great Victoria Street
Belfast BT2 7BA, UK
Phone: +44 28 9020 0991

#3
Katy Daly's
Category: Pub
Average price: £11-25
Address: 17 Ormeau Avenue
Belfast BT2 8HD, UK
Phone: +44 28 9022 2555

#4
The Black Box
Category: Comedy Club, Music Venues
Average price: £11-25
Address: 18-22 Hill Street
Belfast BT1 2LA, UK
Phone: +44 28 9022 4848

#5
John Hewitt
Category: Music Venues, Pub
Average price: Under £10
Address: 51 Donegall Street
Belfast BT2 2FH, UK
Phone: +44 28 9023 0200

#6
Duke Of York
Category: Pub
Average price: £11-25
Address: 7-11 Commercial Court
Belfast BT1 2NB, UK
Phone: +44 28 9023 0295

#7
Empire Music Hall
Category: Pub, Music Venues
Average price: £11-25
Address: 42 Botanic Avenue
Belfast BT7 1JQ, UK
Phone: +44 28 9023 1538

#8
Northern Whig
Category: Pub
Average price: £11-25
Address: 2-10 Bridge Street
Belfast BT1 1LU, UK
Phone: +44 28 9023 2322

#9
Spaniard
Category: Pub, GastroPub
Average price: £26-45
Address: 3 Skipper Street
Belfast BT1 2DZ, UK
Phone: +44 28 9023 2448

#10
Apartment
Category: Pub, European, Lounge
Average price: £11-25
Address: 2 Donegall Square West
Belfast BT1 6JA, UK
Phone: +44 28 9023 2474

#11
Kremlin
Category: Dance Club, Music Venues
Average price: £11-25
Address: 96 Donegall Street
Belfast BT1 2GW, UK
Phone: +44 28 9023 2494

#12
Muriel's
Category: Lounge, European
Average price: £11-25
Address: 12-14 Church Lane
Belfast BT1 4QN, UK
Phone: +44 28 9023 2608

#13
Garrick Bar
Category: Lounge, GastroPub
Average price: £11-25
Address: 29 Chichester Street
Belfast BT1 4JB, UK
Phone: +44 28 9023 3003

#14
White's Tavern
Category: Pub, GastroPub
Average price: £11-25
Address: 2-4 Winecellar Entry
Belfast BT1 1QN, UK
Phone: +44 28 9023 3131

#15
Menagerie Bar
Category: Pub
Average price: Under £10
Address: 130 University Street
Belfast BT7 1HH, UK
Phone: +44 28 9023 3282

#16
Belfast Waterfront Hall
Category: Music Venues
Average price: £11-25
Address: 2 Lanyon Place
Belfast BT13, UK
Phone: +44 28 9023 3768

#17
Morning Star
Category: Pub, Irish
Average price: £11-25
Address: Pottinger's Entry
Belfast BT1 4DU, UK
Phone: +44 28 9023 4520

#18
Pavilion Bar
Category: Pub, Music Venues
Average price: £11-25
Address: 296-298 Ormeau Road
Belfast BT7 2GD, UK
Phone: +44 28 9023 4520

#19
Ryan's Bar & Grill
Category: Bar, British
Average price: £11-25
Address: 116-118 Lisburn Road
Belfast BT9 6AH, UK
Phone: +44 28 9023 4888

#20
The Rotterdam Bar
Category: Music Venues, Pub
Address: 54 Pilot Street
Belfast BT1 3AH, UK
Phone: +44 28 9023 4888

#21
Barking Dog Restaurant
Category: European, British, Wine Bar
Average price: £11-25
Address: 33-35 Malone Road
Belfast BT9 6RU, UK
Phone: +44 28 9023 5678

#22
Molly's Yard
Category: Irish, Pub
Average price: £26-45
Address: 1 College Green Mews
Belfast BT7 1LW, UK
Phone: +44 28 9023 5986

#23
Bittles Bar
Category: Pub
Average price: Under £10
Address: 103 Victoria Street
Belfast BT1 4PB, UK
Phone: +44 28 9023 7173

#24
Kelly's Cellars
Category: Pub, Music Venues
Average price: Under £10
Address: 30-32 Bank Street
Belfast BT1 1, UK
Phone: +44 28 9023 7214

#25
Morning Star
Category: Pub
Average price: Under £10
Address: 17-19 Pottingers Entry
Belfast BT1 4DT, UK
Phone: +44 28 9023 7214

#26
The Cloth Ear
Category: Pub, British
Average price: £11-25
Address: 35 Waring Street
Belfast BT1 2DY, UK
Phone: +44 28 9023 8238

#27
The Botanic Inn
Category: Pub
Average price: £11-25
Address: 23-27 Malone Road
Belfast BT9 6RU, UK
Phone: +44 28 9023 8700

#28
The Errigle Inn
Category: Pub, Coffee & Tea
Average price: £11-25
Address: 312-320 Ormeau Road
Belfast BT7 2GE, UK
Phone: +44 28 9023 9123

#29
McHugh's
Category: Irish, Pub
Average price: £11-25
Address: 29-31 Queens Square
Belfast BT1 3FG, UK
Phone: +44 28 9023 9123

#30
Maddens Bar
Category: Pub, Irish Pub
Average price: £11-25
Address: 74 Smithfield
Belfast BT1 1JE, UK
Phone: +44 28 9023 9163

#31
Union Street
Category: Pub, Dance Club
Average price: £11-25
Address: 8-14 Union Street
Belfast BT1 2JF, UK
Phone: +44 28 9023 9163

#32
The Kitchen Bar
Category: Pub
Average price: £11-25
Address: 1 Victoria Square
Belfast BT1 4QG, UK
Phone: +44 28 9023 9443

#33
Stiff Kitten
Category: Pub
Average price: £11-25
Address: 1 Bankmore Square
Belfast BT7 1DH, UK
Phone: +44 28 9023 9823

#34
The Tap House
Category: Pub
Average price: Under £10
Address: 5-6 Lower Crescent
Belfast BT7 1, UK
Phone: +44 28 9024 1062

#35
AM:PM
Category: Champagne Bar, European
Average price: £11-25
Address: 67-69 Botanic Avenue
Belfast BT7 1, UK
Phone: +44 28 9024 1415

#36
Cafe Vaudeville
Category: Pub
Average price: £26-45
Address: 24-26 Arthur Street
Belfast BT1 4GF, UK
Phone: +44 28 9024 1698

#37
The Parlour
Category: Pub
Average price: £11-25
Address: 2-4 Elmwood Ave
Belfast BT9 6AY, UK
Phone: +44 28 9024 1919

#38
Queens Cafe Bar
Category: Pub, European, Irish
Average price: £11-25
Address: 4 Queens Arcade
Belfast BT1 5FF, UK
Phone: +44 28 9024 2046

#39
The Student's Union at Queens
Category: Music Venues, Lounge
Average price: £11-25
Address: University Road
Belfast BT7 1NF, UK
Phone: +44 28 9024 2414

#40
Eglantine Inn
Category: Pub, Dance Club
Average price: Under £10
Address: 32-40 Malone Road
Belfast BT9 5BQ, UK
Phone: +44 28 9024 2986

#41
Fibber Magees
Category: Bar
Average price: £11-25
Address: 38-40 Great Victoria Street
Belfast BT2 7BA, UK
Phone: +44 28 9024 2986

#42
Basement Bar & Grill
Category: Pub, British, Burgers
Average price: £11-25
Address: 18 Donegall Sq E
Belfast BT1 5HE, UK
Phone: +44 28 9024 3080

#43
Robinsons Bar
Category: Pub
Average price: £11-25
Address: 38 Great Victoria Street
Belfast BT2 7BA, UK
Phone: +44 28 9024 3187

#44
The Kitchen Bar
Category: Pub
Average price: £11-25
Address: 1 Victoria Square
Belfast BT1 4QG, UK
Phone: +44 28 9024 3418

#45
Filthy McNastys
Category: Lounge
Average price: £11-25
Address: 43-35 Dublin Rd
Belfast BT2 7HD, UK
Phone: +44 28 9024 3701

#46
Ronnie Drews
Category: British, Pub
Address: 79-83 May St
Belfast BT1 3JL, UK
Phone: +44 28 9024 4114

#47
Hatfield House
Category: Pub
Average price: Under £10
Address: 130 Ormeau Road
Belfast BT7 2EB, UK
Phone: +44 28 9024 4400

#48
AM:PM
Category: Champagne Bar,
Mediterranean, Lounge
Average price: £11-25
Address: 42 Upper Arthur St
Belfast BT1 4GH, UK
Phone: +44 28 9024 5268

#49
Bar Twelve
Category: Bar
Average price: Under £10
Address: 13 Lower Crescent
Belfast BT7 1, UK
Phone: +44 28 9024 5268

#50
Irene & Nan's
Category: Pub
Average price: £26-45
Address: 1-3 Brunswick St
Belfast BT2 7GE, UK
Phone: +44 28 9024 6058

#51
Bar Bacca
Category: Lounge
Average price: £11-25
Address: 43 Franklin Street
Belfast BT2 7GG, UK
Phone: +44 28 9024 7367

#52
Globe
Category: Pub
Average price: Under £10
Address: 36 University Road
Belfast BT7 1NH, UK
Phone: +44 28 9024 7447

#53
The Bar and Grill
Category: Bar, British
Average price: £26-45
Address: 21 James Street South
Belfast BT2 7GA, UK
Phone: +44 28 9024 7447

#54
Front Page
Category: Pub
Average price: Under £10
Address: 106-110 Donegall St
Belfast BT1 2GX, UK
Phone: +44 28 9024 9009

#55
Frames Complex
Category: Bar, Pool Hall
Average price: Under £10
Address: 2-14 Little Donegall Street
Belfast BT1 2JD, UK
Phone: +44 28 9024 9105

#56
Kings Head
Category: Pub
Average price: £11-25
Address: 829 Lisburn Road
Belfast BT9 7GY, UK
Phone: +44 28 9024 9276

#57
The Edge
Category: Venues, Lounge
Average price: £26-45
Address: Mays Meadows
Belfast BT1 3PH, UK
Phone: +44 28 9026 1809

#58
The Point
Category: Pub
Address: 195-199 Upper
Newtownards Road
Belfast BT4 3JB, UK
Phone: +44 28 9026 2719

#59
Pat's Bar
Category: Pub
Average price: Under £10
Address: 19-22 Princes Dock Street
Belfast BT1 3AA, UK
Phone: +44 28 9027 7000

#60
Deers Head
Category: Pub
Average price: £11-25
Address: Lower Garfield Street
Belfast BT1 1FP, UK
Phone: +44 28 9027 8886

#61
McCrackens
Category: Irish, Pub
Average price: £11-25
Address: 4 Joy's Entry
Belfast BT1 2, UK
Phone: +44 28 9027 9595

#62
The Bridge House - Wetherspoon
Category: British, Pub
Average price: Under £10
Address: 35-43 Bedford St
Belfast BT2 7EJ, UK
Phone: +44 28 9027 9901

#63
Royal Bar
Category: Pub
Address: 188 Sandy Row
Belfast BT12 5EY, UK
Phone: +44 28 9028 3283

#64
Mermaid Inn
Category: Pub
Average price: £11-25
Address: 5-7 Wilsons Court
Belfast BT1 4DQ, UK
Phone: +44 28 9028 5550

#65
Alley Cat
Category: Pub, Burgers
Average price: £11-25
Address: Church Lane
Belfast BT1 4QN, UK
Phone: +44 28 9029 5020

#66
The Chester
Category: British, Pub, Lounge
Average price: £11-25
Address: 466 Antrim Road
Belfast BT15 5GE, UK
Phone: +44 28 9029 8808

#67
The Parador
Category: Pub
Average price: Under £10
Address: 471-473 Ormeau Rd
Belfast BT7 3GR, UK
Phone: +44 28 9029 9600

#68
Bar 7
Category: Pub, Lounge
Average price: £11-25
Address: Queens Quay
Belfast BT3 9QQ, UK
Phone: +44 28 9030 1093

#69
Chelsea Wine Bar
Category: Wine Bar
Average price: £26-45
Address: 344-346 Lisburn Road
Belfast BT9 6GH, UK
Phone: +44 28 9030 1154

#70
Portside Inn
Category: Pub
Average price: £11-25
Address: 1 Dargan Road
Belfast BT3 9JU, UK
Phone: +44 28 9030 1224

#71
21 Social
Category: Bar, Irish, GastroPub
Average price: Under £10
Address: 1 Hill Street
Belfast BT15 1, UK
Phone: +44 28 9030 2807

#72
Monico
Category: Pub
Average price: £11-25
Address: 17 Lombard Street
Belfast BT1 1RB, UK
Phone: +44 28 9030 2984

#73
The Eastender
Category: Pub, British
Average price: £11-25
Address: 426 Woodstock Road
Belfast BT6 9DR, UK
Phone: +44 28 9031 0845

#74
The Sitting Room
Category: Pub
Address: 95 Castle Street
Belfast BT1 1HE, UK
Phone: +44 28 9031 1088

#75
Mynt
Category: Dance Club, GastroPub
Average price: Under £10
Address: 2 -16 Dunbar St
Belfast BT1 2LH, UK
Phone: +44 28 9031 1560

#76
Longfellow Bar
Category: Pub
Address: My Ladys Rd
Belfast BT6 8BZ, UK
Phone: +44 28 9031 2870

#77
Scratch Nightclub
Category: Dance Club, Pub
Average price: Under £10
Address: 5-6 Lower Cresent
Belfast BT7 1NR, UK
Phone: +44 28 9031 4762

#78
Fountain Tavern
Category: Pub
Average price: £11-25
Address: 16 Fountain Street
Belfast BT1 5ED, UK
Phone: +44 28 9031 5264

#79
Le Coop - Made In Belfast
Category: Cocktail Bar, American
Address: 38 Hill Street
Belfast BT1 2LB, UK
Phone: +44 28 9031 6060

#80
Skye
Category: Pub
Address: 21 Howard Street
Belfast BT1 6NB, UK
Phone: +44 28 9031 6060

#81
Dubarry's Bar
Category: Gay Bar
Address: 10 - 14 Gresham St
Belfast BT1 1JN, UK
Phone: +44 28 9031 9955

#82
Rex Bar
Category: Pub
Average price: Under £10
Address: 215 Shankill Road
Belfast BT13 1FQ, UK
Phone: +44 28 9032 0030

#83
Bambu Beach Club
Category: Bar
Average price: £11-25
Address: 2 Queens Quay
Belfast BT3 9QQ, UK
Phone: +44 28 9032 1331

#84
Maverick Bar
Category: Bar
Address: 1 Union Street
Belfast BT1 2JF, UK
Phone: +44 28 9032 1834

#85
Alexander Bar
Category: Pub
Average price: Under £10
Address: 3 York Road
Belfast BT15 3GU, UK
Phone: +44 28 9032 1984

#86
The Hercules Bar
Category: Pub, GastroPub
Average price: Under £10
Address: 61-63 Castle St
Belfast BT1 1GH, UK
Phone: +44 28 9032 1984

#87
Rockies
Category: Sports Bar
Address: 2 Queen's Quay
Belfast BT3 9QQ, UK
Phone: +44 28 9032 2000

#88
Monico Bar
Category: Pub
Average price: Under £10
Address: 17 Lombard Street
Belfast BT1 1RB, UK
Phone: +44 28 9032 2000

#89
The House
Category: Pub, European
Average price: £26-45
Address: 12 Stranmillis Road
Belfast BT9 5AA, UK
Phone: +44 28 9032 2313

#90
Rose & Crown
Category: Pub
Average price: £11-25
Address: 140 Ormeau Road
Belfast BT7 2EB, UK
Phone: +44 28 9032 2600

#91
The Venue
Category: Dance Club
Address: 25-27 Bruce Street
Belfast BT2 7JD, UK
Phone: +44 28 9032 3198

#92
Beaten Docket
Category: Pub
Average price: £11-25
Address: 48 Great Victoria Street
Belfast BT2 7BB, UK
Phone: +44 28 9032 3211

#93
The Beehive
Category: Pub
Average price: Under £10
Address: 193 Falls Rd
Belfast BT12 6FB, UK
Phone: +44 28 9032 3211

#94
Brennan's Bar
Category: Pub
Average price: Under £10
Address: 48-50 Great Victoria St
Belfast BT2 7BB, UK
Phone: +44 28 9032 3313

#95
Cassidy's Bar
Category: Pub
Address: 347-349 Antrim Road
Belfast BT15 2HF, UK
Phone: +44 28 9032 3349

#96
Cutter's Wharf
Category: Restaurant, Lounge
Average price: £11-25
Address: Lockview Road
Belfast BT9 5FJ, UK
Phone: +44 28 9032 3590

#97
V Bar
Category: Pub
Average price: £11-25
Address: 23-31 Shaftesbury Sq
Belfast BT2 7DB, UK
Phone: +44 28 9032 3590

#98
Laganside Inn
Category: Pub
Address: 49 Ravenhill Road
Belfast BT6 8DQ, UK
Phone: +44 28 9032 3741

#99
Red Devil Bar
Category: Pub
Address: 196-198 Falls Rd
Belfast BT12 6AG, UK
Phone: +44 28 9032 3762

#100
4 Corners
Category: Bar
Average price: £11-25
Address: 2-6 Waring St
Belfast BT1 2DX, UK
Phone: +44 28 9032 3900

#101
Copperfields Bar & Restaurant
Category: Pub
Average price: Under £10
Address: 9 Fountain Street
Belfast BT1 5EA, UK
Phone: +44 28 9032 4269

#102
The Phoenix
Category: Pub
Address: 179-181 Antrim Road
Belfast BT15 2GW, UK
Phone: +44 28 9032 4769

#103
The Box
Category: Dance Club
Average price: £26-45
Address: 2 Queen's Quay
Belfast BT3 9QQ, UK
Phone: +44 28 9032 4901

#104
Whitefort
Category: Pub
Average price: £11-25
Address: 61-63 Andersonstown Road
Belfast BT11 9AH, UK
Phone: +44 28 9032 4924

#105
Bert's Jazz Bar
Category: Jazz & Blues
Average price: £11-25
Address: 16 Skipper Street
Belfast BT1 2DZ, UK
Phone: +44 28 9032 5352

#106
McEnaney's
Category: Pub
Address: 1-3 Glen Road
Belfast BT11 8, UK
Phone: +44 28 9032 5968

#107
The Glenowen Inn
Category: Pub
Average price: £11-25
Address: 108/12 Glen Road
Belfast BT11 8BH, UK
Phone: +44 28 9032 6711

#108
Slide Nightclub
Category: Music Venues
Address: Ann St
Belfast BT1 4EF, UK
Phone: +44 28 9032 6711

#109
Brownes Bar & Grill
Category: American, Bar
Average price: Under £10
Address: 91-93 Boucher Road
Belfast BT12 6HR, UK
Phone: +44 28 9032 7007

#110
Biddy Duffy's
Category: Pub
Average price: £11-25
Address: 133c Andersonstown Road
Belfast BT11 9BU, UK
Phone: +44 28 9032 7180

#111
Hole In Wall
Category: Pub
Average price: £11-25
Address: 1 Baltic Avenue
Belfast BT15 2HR, UK
Phone: +44 28 9032 7252

#112
TrenchFoot at Lavery's Bunker
Category: Music Venues
Address: 12-16 Bradbury Place
Belfast BT7 1RS, UK
Phone: +44 28 9032 7308

#113
Aether & Echo
Category: Cocktail Bar
Address: 11 Lower Garfield Street
Belfast BT1 1FP, UK
Phone: +44 28 9032 7829

#114
Hunting Lodge
Category: Pub
Average price: £26-45
Address: Stewartstown Road
Belfast BT11 9FZ, UK
Phone: +44 28 9032 8439

#115
Lifeboat
Category: Bar
Address: 39-41 Custom House Square
Belfast BT1 3FG, UK
Phone: +44 28 9032 9187

#116
The Henry Joy
Category: Pub
Address: 4 The Joy's entry
Belfast BT1 4DR, UK
Phone: +44 28 9032 9310

#117
Event Horizon
Category: Gay Bar
Address: Union St
Belfast BT1 2JF, UK
Phone: +44 28 9033 1174

#118
P. McLaughlin Bar
Category: Pub
Address: 150 Antrim Rd
Belfast BT15 2GW, UK
Phone: +44 28 9033 1528

#119
American Bar
Category: Pub
Address: 65-65a Dock Street
Belfast BT15 1LF, UK
Phone: +44 28 9033 1925

#120
Rain
Category: Dance Club
Average price: £26-45
Address: 10-14 Tomb St
Belfast BT1 3AS, UK
Phone: +44 28 9033 2121

#121
Patrick Mclaughlin & Co
Category: Pub
Address: 150 Duncairn Gardens
Belfast BT15 2GN, UK
Phone: +44 28 9033 2445

#122
Felons Club
Category: Lounge
Address: 537 Falls Road
Belfast BT11 9AB, UK
Phone: +44 28 9033 3003

#123
Cuckoo Belfast
Category: Pub
Address: 149 Lisburn Road
Belfast BT9 7AJ, UK
Phone: +44 28 9033 3388

#124
Cosgrove Bar
Category: Wine Bar
Average price: £11-25
Address: 34 King Street
Belfast BT1 6AD, UK
Phone: +44 28 9033 3905

#125
Speakeasy Bar
Category: Pub
Address: 77-79 University Road
Belfast BT7 1GX, UK
Phone: +44 28 9033 4400

#126
Rock Bar
Category: Pub
Address: 491 Falls Road
Belfast BT12 6DE, UK
Phone: +44 28 9035 1625

#127
Mono
Category: Dance Club
Average price: Under £10
Address: 100 Ann Street
Belfast BT1 3HH, UK
Phone: +44 28 9037 0305

#128
McElhatton's
Category: Beer, Wine & Spirits, Bar
Address: 106-110 Donegall Street
Belfast BT1 2GX, UK
Phone: +44 28 9037 0314

#129
Shisha Lounge
Category: Lounge, Tapas Bar
Address: 211 Lisburn Rd
Belfast BT9 7AP, UK
Phone: +44 28 903726

#130
Victoria's
Category: Pub
Address: 81 Chichester Street
Belfast BT1 4JE, UK
Phone: +44 28 9038 1111

#131
Monzu
Category: Italian, Bar
Average price: £11-25
Address: 701 Lisburn Road
Belfast BT9 7GU, UK
Phone: +44 28 9038 1931

#132
Portside Inn
Category: Pub, Breakfast & Brunch
Average price: £11-25
Address: 1 Dargan Road
Belfast BT3 9JU, UK
Phone: +44 28 9038 1994

#133
Ollie's
Category: Dance Club
Average price: £26-45
Address: 35-39 Waring St
Belfast BT1 2DY, UK
Phone: +44 28 9039 7788

#134
W5 At Odyssey
Category: Pub, Food
Address: Odyssey 2 Queens Quays
Belfast BT3 9QQ, UK
Phone: +44 28 9039 7788

#135
The Devenish
Category: Pub
Address: 33 - 37 Finaghy Road N
Belfast BT10 0JB, UK
Phone: +44 28 9042 2588

#136
Thompsons Garage
Category: Bar
Average price: Under £10
Address: 3 Pattersons Place
Belfast BT1 4HW, UK
Phone: +44 28 9042 4759

#137
The Albany
Category: Restaurant, Pub
Address: 701-703 Lisburn Road
Belfast BT9 7GU, UK
Phone: +44 28 9042 7439

#138
Old Mill
Category: Pub
Address: Good Shepherd Road
Belfast BT17 0PP, UK
Phone: +44 28 9043 8764

#139
Weatherspoons
Category: Pub
Address: 37 Bedford Street
Belfast BT2 7EJ, UK
Phone: +44 28 9043 9160

#140
Trocadero Bar
Category: Pub
Address: 157 Cromac Street
Belfast BT2 8JE, UK
Phone: +44 28 9044 2080

#141
Wellington Park Hotel
Category: Hotel, Lounge
Average price: £11-25
Address: 21 Malone Road
Belfast BT9 6RU, UK
Phone: +44 28 9044 8446

#142
Elbow Rooms
Category: Pub
Address: 45 Dublin Road
Belfast BT2 7HD, UK
Phone: +44 28 9044 9863

#143
Dempfey's
Category: Pub
Address: 45 Dublin Road
Belfast BT2 7HD, UK
Phone: +44 28 9045 0450

#144
Christopher's Taverns
Category: Pub
Address: 141 Donegall Pass
Belfast BT7 1DS, UK
Phone: +44 28 9045 1990

#145
M Club
Category: Dance Club
Average price: £11-25
Address: 31 Bradbury Place
Belfast BT7 1RR, UK
Phone: +44 28 9045 4440

#146
Crown Liquor Saloon
Category: Pub
Address: 46 Great Victoria Street
Belfast BT2 7BA, UK
Phone: +44 28 9045 5654

#147
Garrick Bar
Category: Pub
Address: 29-33 Montgomery Street
Belfast BT1 4NX, UK
Phone: +44 28 9045 6118

#148
Yello
Category: Dance Club
Address: 2-16 Dunbar St
Belfast BT1 2LH, UK
Phone: +44 28 9045 7166

#149
Magennis Bar
Category: Pub
Address: 83 May Street
Belfast BT1 3JL, UK
Phone: +44 28 9045 7215

#150
Nicholl's Bar Brasserie
Category: Pub
Address: 12-14 Church Lane
Belfast BT1 4QN, UK
Phone: +44 28 9045 7534

#151
Belfast Music Week
Category: Festival, Music Venues
Address: Studio ON 2 School Rd
Belfast BT5 7UA, UK
Phone: +44 28 9045 8178

#152
Factory Bar & Grill
Category: Pub
Address: 10-12 Gresham Street
Belfast BT1 1JN, UK
Phone: +44 28 9045 8379

#153
The Advocate Bar
Category: Wine Bar
Average price: Under £10
Address: 81-85 Chichester St
Belfast BT1 4JE, UK
Phone: +44 28 9046 0011

#154
Cosy Bar
Category: Bar
Address: 44 Omeath St
Belfast BT6 8, UK
Phone: +44 28 9046 7020

#155
Oasis Bar
Category: Pub
Address: 58 Distillery Street
Belfast BT12 5BJ, UK
Phone: +44 28 9046 7070

#156
Wineins Public House
Category: Pub
Address: 2-4 Elmwood Avenue
Belfast BT9 6AY, UK
Phone: +44 28 9046 7080

#157
The Kitchen Bar
Category: Bar
Address: 1 Victoria Square
Belfast BT1 4QG, UK
Phone: +44 28 9046 7788

#158
Sunflower Pub
Category: Pub
Address: 65 Union Street
Belfast BT1 2FP, UK
Phone: +44 28 9047 2977

#159
Gracemount Enterprises
Category: Pub
Address: 2 - 14 Little Donegall Street
Belfast BT1 2JD, UK
Phone: +44 28 9047 3446

#160
My Lady's Inn
Category: Pub
Address: 36 My Ladys Road
Belfast BT6 8FB, UK
Phone: +44 28 9049 1883

#161
SQ Bar & Grill
Category: Wine Bar
Address: 20 Talbot Street
Belfast BT1 2LD, UK
Phone: +44 28 9050 1888

#162
Koyote Oddissey
Category: Pub
Address: 2 Queens Quay
Belfast BT3 9QQ, UK
Phone: +44 28 9050 9740

#163
Flame
Category: Bistro, Bar
Address: 46 Howard Street
Belfast BT1 6PG, UK
Phone: +44 28 9050 9750

#164
Laurel Leaf
Category: Pub
Address: 155 Northumberland Street
Belfast BT13 2JF, UK
Phone: +44 28 9050 9750

#165
Diamond Jubilee
Category: Pub
Address: 150-152 Peters Hill
Belfast BT13 2AD, UK
Phone: +44 28 9050 9750

#166
Four In Hand
Category: Pub
Address: 116-118 Lisburn Road
Belfast BT9 6AH, UK
Phone: +44 28 9050 9777

#167
Molly Maguires
Category: Pub
Address: 120 Great Georges Street
Belfast BT15 1FH, UK
Phone: +44 28 9050 9840

#168
Celtic Bar
Category: Pub
Address: 91 Falls Road
Belfast BT12 4PE, UK
Phone: +44 28 9050 9850

#169
Cook Inn
Category: Pub
Address: 11a Sandringham Street
Belfast BT9 7DR, UK
Phone: +44 28 9050 9888

#170
The Hudson Bar
Category: Bar, Chicken Wings
Address: 10 Gresham Street
Belfast BT1 1JN, UK
Phone: +44 28 9050 9950

#171
Clarandon Bar
Category: Pub
Address: 29 Garmoyle Street
Belfast BT15 1DY, UK
Phone: +44 28 9050 9999

#172
Royal Bar
Category: Pub
Address: 237 Shankill Road
Belfast BT13 1FR, UK
Phone: +44 28 9058 0777

#173
Berlin Arms
Category: Pub
Address: 265 Shankill Road
Belfast BT13 1FR, UK
Phone: +44 28 9059 3700

#174
Laughter Lounge
Category: Comedy Club
Address: Odyssey Pavillion
Belfast BT3 9QQ, UK
Phone: +44 28 9059 6666

#175
Bia Beatha
Category: Pub
Address: 145 Falls Road
Belfast BT12 6AF, UK
Phone: +44 28 9060 0479

#176
Big House
Category: Pub
Address: 296-298 Ormeau Road
Belfast BT7 2GB, UK
Phone: +44 28 9060 2210

#177
Cock & Hen
Category: Pub
Address: 3 Lord Street
Belfast BT5 4QG, UK
Phone: +44 28 9060 2675

#178
Mountainview Tavern
Category: Pub
Address: Shankill Road
Belfast BT13 3AG, UK
Phone: +44 28 9060 3790

#179
Park Plaza
Category: Bar
Address: Belfast International Airport
Belfast, UK
Phone: +44 28 9061 0070

#180
Cafferys Bar
Category: Pub
Address: 193 Falls Road
Belfast BT12 6FB, UK
Phone: +44 28 9061 1653

#181
Festival Of Fools
Category: Bar
Address: 23-25 Gordon Street
Belfast BT12 6DL, UK
Phone: +44 28 9061 3951

#182
King Richard Tavern
Category: Pub
Address: 10 Castlereagh Road
Belfast BT5 5FP, UK
Phone: +44 28 9061 4085

#183
Gallaghers Bar
Category: Pub
Address: York Gate Shopping Centre
Belfast BT15 1WA, UK
Phone: +44 28 9061 9875

#184
The Fly
Category: Restaurant, Dance Club
Address: 5-6 Lower Cresent
Belfast BT7 1NR, UK
Phone: +44 28 9062 1841

#185
Mercury Bar & Grill
Category: Pub
Address: 451 Ormeau Road
Belfast BT7 3GQ, UK
Phone: +44 28 9062 7496

#186
Cables Bar
Category: British, Lounge
Address: 4 Lanyon Place
Belfast BT1 3LP, UK
Phone: +44 28 9062 8098

#187
The Stadium Bar
Category: Pub
Address: 346 Shankill Road
Belfast BT13 3AB, UK
Phone: +44 28 9062 9480

#188
Great Eastern
Category: Pub
Address: 273 Newtownards Road
Belfast BT4 1AF, UK
Phone: +44 28 9064 1410

#189
The Mount Inn
Category: Pub
Address: 156 North Queen Street
Belfast BT15 1HQ, UK
Phone: +44 28 9064 9017

#190
Hunters
Category: Pub
Address: Lisburn Road
Belfast BT9 7AJ, UK
Phone: +44 28 9064 9297

#191
Prince Albert Lounge
Category: Pub
Address: 369 Newtownards Road
Belfast BT4 1AJ, UK
Phone: +44 28 9066 0995

#192
The Times Bar
Category: Pub
Address: 24-28 York Road
Belfast BT15 3HE, UK
Phone: +44 28 9066 1522

#193
Henry Joys
Category: Pub
Address: 167-177 Oldpark Road
Belfast BT14 6QP, UK
Phone: +44 28 9066 1885

#194
The Green Dragon
Category: Pub
Address: 345 Antrim Road
Belfast BT15 2HF, UK
Phone: +44 28 9066 3388

#195
Westway Snooker Hall
Category: Pool Hall
Average price: Under £10
Address: 557 Falls Road
Belfast BT11 9AB, UK
Phone: +44 28 9066 4442

#196
Rossetta Bar
Category: Pub
Address: 73-75 Rosetta Road
Belfast BT6 0LR, UK
Phone: +44 28 9066 4442

#197
32 North
Category: Pub
Address: 475 Crumlin Road
Belfast BT14 7GA, UK
Phone: +44 28 9066 5103

#198
Grove Tavern
Category: Pub
Address: 203 York Road
Belfast BT15 3HB, UK
Phone: +44 28 9066 5225

#199
Sliabh Dubh Bar
Category: Pub
Address: Whiterock Road
Belfast BT12 7FW, UK
Phone: +44 28 9066 7776

#200
Fiddler's Inn
Category: Bar
Address: 11 Kennedy Way
Belfast BT11 9AP, UK
Phone: +44 28 9066 8019

#201
Shine Productions
Category: Bar
Average price: £26-45
Address: 1 Bankmore Square
Belfast BT7 1DH, UK
Phone: +44 28 9068 2266

#202
The Hedgehog & Bucket
Category: Pub
Address: 536-538 Oldpark Road
Belfast BT14 6QJ, UK
Phone: +44 28 9068 2266

#203
Us Inns
Category: Pub
Address: 2 Holland Drive
Belfast BT5 6EH, UK
Phone: +44 28 9068 6970

#204
Sliabh Dubh
Category: Pub
Address: 703-705 Springfield Road
Belfast BT12 7FP, UK
Phone: +44 28 9068 6970

#205
Cavehill Inn
Category: Pub
Address: Cavehill Road
Belfast BT15 5BP, UK
Phone: +44 28 9068 7177

#206
Maginty's Bar & Restaurant
Category: Pub
Address: 466 Antrim Road
Belfast BT15 5GE, UK
Phone: +44 28 9069 3193

#207
Trinity Lodge
Category: Pub
Address: Monagh Grove
Belfast BT11 8EJ, UK
Phone: +44 28 9072 1000

#208
Cafe Zint
Category: Wine Bar
Address: 12 Stranmillis Road
Belfast BT9 5AA, UK
Phone: +44 28 9072 7890

#209
Beechill Inns
Category: Pub
Address: Cedarhurst Road
Belfast BT8 7RH, UK
Phone: +44 28 9073 1303

#210
Queens Inn
Category: Pub
Address: Kings Square
Belfast BT5 7EA, UK
Phone: +44 28 9073 1404

#211
Suffolk Inn
Category: Pub
Address: Suffolk Road
Belfast BT11 9PE, UK
Phone: +44 28 9073 2443

#212
Mcgrath's Bar
Category: Wine Bar
Address: 78 Cliftonville Road
Belfast BT14 6JZ, UK
Phone: +44 28 9074 1769

#213
Dunmurry Inn
Category: Pub
Address: 195 Kingsway
Belfast BT17 9SB, UK
Phone: +44 28 9074 2838

#214
Silver Inn
Category: Pub
Address: 222 Stewartstown Road
Belfast BT17 0LB, UK
Phone: +44 28 9074 3377

#215
Eivissa
Category: Dance Club
Address: 43 Franklin Street
Belfast BT2, UK
Phone: +44 28 9074 3806

#216
The Dirty Duck
Category: Pub, Restaurant
Average price: £11-25
Address: 3 Kinnegar Road
Holywood BT18 9JN, UK
Phone: +44 28 9074 3806

#217
The Maypole
Category: Pub
Average price: £11-25
Address: 55 High Street
Holywood BT18 9AB, UK
Phone: +44 28 9074 4484

#218
The Frisky Bear
Category: Pub
Address: 62 High Street
Holywood BT18 9, UK
Phone: +44 28 9074 4524

#219
El Divino
Category: Dance Club
Address: Mays Meadow
Belfast BT1 3PH, UK
Phone: +44 28 9074 6021

#220
The Attik Café Bar
Category: Pub
Address: 62a High St
Holywood BT18 9AE, UK
Phone: +44 28 9074 7494

#221
Auld House
Category: Pub
Address: 27 Church Road
Newtownards BT23 6BB, UK
Phone: +44 28 9074 9179

#222
The Limelight
Category: Music Venues
Average price: Under £10
Address: 17 Ormeau Avenue
Belfast BT2 8HD, UK
Phone: +44 28 9075 2506

#223
Morrisons Lounge Bar
Category: Pub
Average price: £11-25
Address: 21 Bedford Street
Belfast BT2 7EJ, UK
Phone: +44 28 9075 3432

#224
Fountain Bar
Category: Pub
Average price: Under £10
Address: 880 Shore Rd
Newtownabbey BT36 7DQ, UK
Phone: +44 28 9077 1422

#225
Sunrise Hot Food Bar
Category: Wine Bar
Address: 40 Cregagh Road
Belfast BT6 9EQ, UK
Phone: +44 28 9077 1422

#226
McGlone's Bar
Category: Pub
Address: 131-133 Kingsway Dunmurry
Dunmurry BT17 9RY, UK
Phone: +44 28 9077 1610

#227
King's Hall
Category: Music Venues
Average price: £26-45
Address: Balmoral
Belfast BT9 6GU, UK
Phone: +44 28 9077 9376

#228
Bentley's Of Holywood
Category: Pub
Address: 62a High Street
Holywood BT18 9AE, UK
Phone: +44 28 9077 9376

#229
Dempseys International
Category: Bar
Address: 45 Dublin Road
Belfast BT2 7HD, UK
Phone: +44 28 9079 2395

#230
The Blackstaff Bar
Category: Wine Bar
Address: 149 Springfield Road
Belfast BT12 7DA, UK
Phone: +44 28 9080 5552

#231
National Club
Category: Pool Hall
Address: 19 Queen Street
Belfast BT1 6EA, UK
Phone: +44 28 9080 7111

#232
P & F Amusements
Category: Amusement Park, Bar
Address: Unit 9 Graham Ind Est Dargan
Belfast BT3 9JP, UK
Phone: +44 28 9086 4353

#233
Pinc Retail
Category: Music Venues
Address: 18-22 Hill Street
Belfast BT1 2LA, UK
Phone: +44 28 9087 1106

#234
Andersonstown Social Club
Category: Bar
Address: 38-40 South Link
Belfast BT11 8GX, UK
Phone: +44 28 9092 1920

#235
Michael Dwyers
Category: Bar
Address: 303 Grosvenor Road
Belfast BT12 4LL, UK
Phone: +44 28 9097 3726

#236
Platform Holywood
Category: British, Bar
Address: 29 Hibernia Street
Holywood BT18 9JE, UK
Phone: +44 28 9445 7000

#237
Pot Black Snooker Hall
Category: Pool Hall
Address: 79 Springfield Road
Belfast BT12 7AE, UK
Phone: +44 28 9545 8120

#238
Qe 1 Snooker Club
Category: Pool Hall
Address: 32-46 Castlereagh Road
Belfast BT5 5FP, UK
Phone: +44 28 9560 0700

#239
DJ George Welsh
Category: Bar, Social Club
Address: 3 Lochinver Drive
Castlereagh BT5 7AJ, UK
Phone: +44 4428 9024 6925

#240
Manor Snooker Club
Category: Pool Hall
Address: 701a Lisburn Road
Belfast BT9 7GU, UK
Phone: +44 7767 603279

#241
Eclipse Disco Centre
Category: Bar
Address: 143-145 Upper
Newtownards Road
Belfast BT4 3HX, UK
Phone: +44 7769 924360

#242
Brook Lodge Bar
Category: Wine Bar
Address: Summerhill Drive
Belfast BT17 0RE, UK
Phone: +44 7933 901933

#243
Csimiparty
Category: Music Venues
Address: 88 North Road
Belfast BT4 3DJ, UK
Phone: +44 7973 631183

#244
Grand Opera House
Category: Music Venues
Average price: £26-45
Address: Great Victoria Street
Belfast BT2 7HR, UK
Phone: +44 870 423 6492

#245
Catch My Pal
Category: Pool Hall
Address: 191a Kingsway
Belfast BT17 9RY, UK

#246
Oh Yeah Music Centre
Category: Music Venues
Address: 15-21 Gordon Street
Belfast BT1 2LG, UK

#247
Ulster Hall
Category: Performing Arts, Music Venues
Average price: £11-25
Address: Bedford Street
Belfast BT2 7FF, UK

#248
Botanic Gardens
Category: Park, Music Venues
Address: Botanic Avenue
Belfast BT7 1LP, UK

#249
Drumbo Park Greyhound Stadium
Category: Bar
Address: 57 Ballyskeagh Road
Lambeg Lisburn BT27 5TE, UK

#250
Villa Italia
Category: Bar
Average price: £11-25
Address: 37-41 University Road
Belfast BT7 1ND, UK
Phone: +44 28 9032 8356

Printed in Great Britain
by Amazon